The Slingshot Syndrome

The Slingshot Syndrome

Why America's Leading Technology Firms Fail at Innovation

Reid McRae Watts

Writers Club Press

San Jose New York Lincoln Shanghai

The Slingshot Syndrome
Why America's Leading Technology Firms Fail at Innovation

Writers Club Press
an imprint of iUniverse, Inc.

For information address:
iUniverse, Inc.
5220 S. 16th St., Suite 200
Lincoln, NE 68512
www.iuniverse.com

The Prologue and Chapter 9 are works of fiction. All events, locations,
institutions, themes, persons, characters and plots in those chapters are
completely fictional. Any resemblance to places or persons, living or deceased
are of the invention of the author.

ISBN: 0-595-20813-4

Printed in the United States of America

To Therese

Epigraph

Slingshot Syndrome—(n): A pattern where startups with little resources utilize their natural ability to rapidly innovate and commercialize new-to-the-world products to replace large, mature, market-leading corporations. The Slingshot Syndrome was first established in the computer industry in the 1980's and continues today in the computer, communications equipment, and software industries exemplifying the "Creative Destruction" cycle predicted by the economist Joseph Schumpeter. The syndrome appears to be particularly successful when the markets involved are being disrupted by rapid technological change, which places a premium on rapid commercialization of new technology. The term is derived from the biblical story of David and Goliath where David slayed the arrogant, heavily armored and unsuspecting giant Goliath with a mere slingshot.

Contents

Acknowledgements xi

Introduction xiii

Prologue A day in the life of a CEO, 2008 1

Chapter 1 Losing the Leadership: How the Information Technology Leaders of the 1980's Lost their Leadership by 2001 13

Chapter 2 Capital Markets: the Polarization of Patient and Impatient Money 26

Chapter 3 Speed of Change: Past and Future Speed of Change in the Information Technologies 35

Chapter 4 Traditional vs. Startup: Comparing IT Company Structures, Controls, and Systems 46

Chapter 5 Solutions Analysis: Why the Previous Attempts to Solve the Problem have Failed 58

Chapter 6 The Solution to the Slingshot Syndrome: What to Do to Get the Best of Both the Corporate and the Startup Worlds 70

Chapter 7 The Communications Industry: Goliaths at Risk 93

Chapter 8 Paths of Migration: How Do We Get There? 105

Chapter 9 Tales of the Transition 119

Chapter 10 Implications of the Future Corporation 149

Chapter 11 Actions for You to Take Today 158

About the Author 167

Glossary 171

Acknowledgements

Special recognition should go to Virginia Hunt of Progeny Ventures, who composed the fictional stories in the Prologue and Chapter 9. Although I provided her with the material for the stories, she created the plots, characters, and stories, and wrote the prose. Virginia also helped edit the rest of the book, improving the prose, critiquing the chapters, doing some of the research, etc.

DeWitt Bowman, retired Chief Investment Officer of CalPERS, reviewed my thesis on how pension funds such as CalPERS manage their investments and provided some invaluable insights and corrections. Dennis Roberson, CTO of Motorola, deserves credit for getting me to analyze technology trends. Steve Socolof, Strategy and Business Development VP at Lucent, introduced me to the concept of corporate venture capital and incubators and reviewed the sections on Lucent's New Venture Group activities. Marcus Morton, President of Absolute Entertainment, reviewed and corrected the description on how the film industry is structured.

Special thanks to those who reviewed the manuscript and gave me valuable feedback. This includes Daniel Greenberg of James Levine, Dan Dvorak of NASA's Jet Propulsion Lab, editor and author John D. W. Watts, Covad Chief Architect and VP of Engineering Greg Wetzel, Lucent's Director of Intellectual Property and Technology Management Terry McPherson, Managing Partner of Sarnoff's nVention subsidiary Norman Winarsky, Sarnoff's Director of Corporate and Market Communications Tom Lento, the former head of Xerox's corporate venture fund and current General Partner of the Israel Infinity Fund Kenneth Rind, and Dennis Neufarth.

Introduction

Depending on your background and a familiarity with the different subjects covered in this book, you may want to read the chapters in a different order. I wrote the book so that each chapter stands alone, and they can be read in any order. Although reading it straight through is likely to be the best approach for most readers, some readers may find it much more comprehensible, interesting, and enjoyable to read the chapters out of order. Here are a few suggestions for doing that.

The first thing to note is that this book is unusual in that it contains two categories of chapters: fictional and non-fictional. The fictional chapters are the Prologue and Chapter 9. The purpose of the fictional chapters is to allow the reader to experience, via the fictional characters, the future that this book foresees. The purpose of the non-fictional chapters is to analyze the issues with which the information technology industry has been dealing with respect to new technology. Based on that analysis, the non-fictional chapters explain the current turmoil within the information technology industry, project where it will lead, and the effects it will have on you.

Chapter 1 gives historical evidence for the key problem and Chapter 6 proposes the solution. If you find the technical jargon in Chapter 1 a bit hard to follow, don't worry—it is not essential in your understanding of the rest of the book. Do note that there is a Glossary at the end of the book that defines most of the terms used. Chapters 2 through 5 analyze the problem from different vantagepoints, while Chapters 8 and 10 recommend what corporations should do now to solve the problem. Chapter 11 recommends what you as an individual should do knowing where the industry is headed. Chapter 7 is an in-depth analysis of the communications industry, a segment of the information technology industry which is currently in the greatest turmoil, yet has the most promise.

If you are reading the non-fictional chapters and start to bog down in the subject matter, I suggest reading a few of the fictional stories in Chapter 9 before proceeding. Some readers may wish to read the fictional stories in the Prologue and Chapter 9 first and then read the rest of the book. Others may want to skip the fictional stories altogether. Read in any order, the book should provide some education, insights and ideas of what actions to take to survive and prosper is this exciting period of technological innovation.

If you would like to comment on the material in this book, please visit my web site at www.progenyvc.com/slingshot and add your comments under the "Comments" page. While there you can also view quotes from other readers and stay up-to-date with events related to this book.

Prologue

A day in the life of a CEO, 2008

* A fictional story based on the non-fictional problem analyses and solutions discussed in Chapters 1 - 11

Mary Anne Porter, CEO and chairman of the board left her tennis bag at home today, unlike most Fridays of the past six and a half years. Friday afternoons were reserved for tennis, Mary Anne's sport of choice, which contributed greatly to her mental clarity; however, not this Friday. Something more important was at hand that required her uninterrupted attentions. She reclined in her beige leather chair behind her cherry desk and contemplated how the events of the day might ensue. Her auburn hair was evenly cut just below her jaw line, a cut that exposed her high cheekbones and light green eyes to the morning sun, which shined relentlessly through the double paned bay windows atop the fifth floor of the company's Chicago headquarters. She certainly wasn't the typical CEO, but then again, this company had needed someone more than just typical to survive: they had needed someone extraordinary. The squeaking noise made by her chair couldn't distract her from her state of deep thought.

It is almost 7:30AM, the board meeting is less than an hour and a half away. I had no idea I would be this nervous.

The paperclip she had been anxiously twisting was now bent and deemed completely unusable.

That's OK, I don't use paper that much anyway.

She tossed it carelessly behind her into the wastebasket. This meeting would determine the success or failure of the company, as well as would determine her level of participation in its future.

I am too deeply associated with the plan, too much of me is ingrained in the proposal. If they don't want to risk it, then they're saying they aren't willing to bet on me.

Mary Anne knew that this meeting would decide her future as the CEO of M. Collins Corporation. She knew her proposal to the board was risky, much like her plan of six years before, and she did not let that intimidate her then. She certainly wasn't about to start now.

Mary Anne was interrupted from her thoughts by the shrill ring of her telephone.

I knew I should have turned that thing off.

Mary Anne recognized the number and answered it without further hesitation. "George. Thank God. Where are you? I need you at this meeting at 9. Can you make it back in time? Yes, I know you are in the air…You land at what time?"

Mary Anne grimaced with anguish, "George, that is really cutting it close. You know how important this meeting is. Couldn't you have gotten on an earlier flight? Ok, I know you tried. I'll have Melissa send a car to O'Hare to fetch you. Oh—right, right. Meridian Airlines does that for you. Fine. Oh, did you get the presentation outline? I just sent it a few minutes ago…and?"

Mary Anne shifted her weight from her left heel to her right as she waited briefly for his response. She returned a smile that indicated George's satisfactory reply.

"I knew you would think so, George. See you in an hour."

George Sand, CFO, was arriving from Dallas, Texas a half-hour before the board meeting, and Mary Anne knew that he would barely make it in time. She had insisted on him rearranging his flight to come back to head-quarters instead of participating virtually; he was much more of a mental support beam in person than on the wire. George had been a loyal sup-porter of her plan since her CEO tenure began in 2002. If it hadn't been for George's support, as well as the support of Martin Gregory, a former venture capitalist on the board of directors, Mary Anne Porter may not have ever been appointed to the CEO position at M. Collins Corporation and more importantly, she would have faced certain resistance against her implementation and would have never been able to execute the changes that the company desperately needed at the time.

Under Mary Anne's stewardship, the company had experienced a com-plete turnaround. Now, six years later, it was a high-flying and profitable company of $25 billion with an expected 20% increase in earnings annu-ally. Nothing short of a miracle, as Forbes described it in 2004. Only three years prior, Forbes, and virtually all of the media, penned the company for dead. With an ailing computer division, losses plunging the company fur-ther into debt, their credit rating at a notch above junk bond status, and no promising future in sight, the company was for all intents and purposes abandoned. It would have been left for dead, had not this innovative, for-mer venture capitalist, and daughter of a famous film mogul taken the reigns of the information technology giant and assumed the challenge, a challenge deemed impossible by her predecessors. She accepted the com-plex task on one condition: that she be able to implement her changes, regardless of how radical they may seem at the time, all the way through to the end. Now, 2008, the time has come to complete the transition, to fin-ish the disintegration of the company, now that enough evidence existed to support her theory on how the company should be structured to opti-mize technological change; however, it would be more difficult to com-plete the transition than it had been to execute it six years earlier. With the recent success of the company, the board felt that they had more to lose and more to sacrifice if the strategic decision was wrong.

Six years before, it was all or nothing because almost nothing was left, nothing other than a small amount of capital from the liquidation of assets and, what saved the company, their strong international sales force. The board, as well as the shareholders, owed her their gratitude and their support, despite how difficult it was for her to convince them of the essential, revolutionary changes that ultimately saved the company.

At 8:55 AM, as she slipped into her matching cream blazer, Mary Anne gathered her notes and coffee mug as she headed down the hall into the boardroom. Her navy blue silk blouse, which contrasted nicely with her auburn hair, was the perfect texture for this warm spring morning. After all, boardrooms could get rather heated at times and Mary Anne knew this first hand. The virtual meeting was to take place in less than five minutes and George had still not arrived, yet another reason for her to prematurely perspire. As she passed by her administrative assistant's desk, she picked up an extra company pen, silver logo embossed on the front, for George of course. He always forgot to bring a pen.

He definitely needs one for this meeting.

She tucked any escaping corners of her blouse into the waist of her skirt as she made her way to the front of the large conference room, coffee mug and loose papers nestled safely in her free hand.

Mary Anne opened the large oak doors of the virtual boardroom. It looked so different from nearly six years earlier when she had made her original proposal. The dark glass topped cherry table and the bay windows were the only items in the room that remained the same. The pull down screen for projection had been replaced with a 10' x 10' virtual screen, with box separators to classify different participants. Mary Anne noticed that only Mark Sayberg had checked in.

In Mary Anne's opinion, Mark was certainly a skeptic of her plans. At times, it seemed he was arguing and disagreeing with her strategy for disagreement's sake, although Mary Anne appreciated his alternative view.

I have never in my life learned anything from any man who agreed with me.

She would remind herself of this to avoid any rude or inappropriate outbursts on her behalf directed squarely at Mark and his seemingly pointless resistance. To Mark's credit, he almost always succumbed to reason and logic and allowed her to make her changes after he had time to consider the alternatives.

At least he forces me think about the way I was doing things and the reasons for them. And for that, she appreciated his opposition.

Just as the last board member logged on, George rushed into the seat beside her, notepad in hand. "George, so glad you could make it."

Mary Anne glanced in his direction as he patted his lapel in search of a writing utensil. The CEO handed him the pen as she smiled, "Shall we begin now, George?" He nodded in agreement as she pressed the remote to log onto the meeting.

As at all of their monthly board meetings, this one was no exception to formality. The Secretary of the Board Timothy Bryant, also chief legal counsel, called the meeting to order and then handed the floor off to the chairman, Ms. Mary Anne Porter. Mary Anne opened the meeting with her usual greeting: "Good morning everyone, how is the weather in your respective locations?"

The seven board members responded with moderate enthusiasm. She always began the meetings this way to restore a sense of intimacy that the virtual meetings eliminated in exchange for lower travel costs and convenience, and also to take note as to where everyone was located should a face-to-face assembly be necessary.

"I am pleased to see that each of you are able to make it this morning. Kevin Melbourne, you must be exhausted, it is nearly Midnight in Tokyo. Thank you all for sacrificing your time. We need to discuss something of great importance for the continued success of the company and I need you all here for it. I trust you each have the presentation?" A confirmation from each assured her that each member had reviewed her proposal and, as she had anticipated, each had questions.

"Let me first go over the presentation, and since it has been reviewed by all, please feel free to interrupt me with your questions."

The first point Mary Anne approached was a sensitive one, and she knew it.

"The time has come for the company to spin off 60% to 80% of the ownership of the core business units into the public markets through a spin off directly to the shareholders. I expect this to be completed by the end of the summer and in enough time to show up on next year's annual report."

For a brief moment no one spoke. The business units were the last major step needed to fully convert the company into a distribution company, fueled by a network of startup "single product" companies. Spinning the business units out would be the mental admission of this fact, and for a few of the board members, and certainly the business unit leaders, it would be tough to take.

Hugh Garrison, a fifty-five year old former CEO and long time board member representing M. Collins Corporation's institutional investor CalPERS, spoke first. "Mary Anne, the business units are doing well now, *inside* of the company. Their current products are at a growth stage and they serve our markets well, and profitably. Spinning them out as independent companies will expose them to our competitors. We would be relinquishing control of our key product divisions—the core of our company. We can't let that happen, Mary Anne. I'm sorry. We trusted you in the past, and you have performed well for us, so I am willing to hear you out. Can you tell us why this makes any sense at all?"

Mary Anne anticipated this kind of reaction; she had dealt with it many times in the past. "Hugh, I understand your point, and I appreciate your perspective. This is a long-term move for the company, but it will have immediate, short-term effects as well. With respect to making any sense, it makes perfect sense, if you can see the strategic move from a uncommon angle. Here is some additional information that you may not be aware of:

we estimate that by spinning out our core business units, their sales will increase by over 20%.—George, what is the pro forma on that?"

"Well, Ms. Porter," the CFO said with sincere reverence, "we are looking at 20% increase in the first year, then up to 50% increase in 3 years, pre-maturation, which are of course conservative estimates based on our discussions with the other distribution channels."

Hugh sat back in his chair with the new information. Mary Anne continued, "Hugh, the business units' per-unit costs will drop considerably due to the economies of scale. Up to a point, much of their costs are essentially fixed. Therefore, each incremental sale is almost pure incremental profit. By spinning out the product business units, they will be able to credibly access horizontal markets where we do not play because of our vertical market focus. The increased sales volume will have the effect of decreasing unit costs and thereby increasing margins. We will get part of the unit cost decrease as a cost decrease to our sales channel, thereby increasing our margins and increasing our flexibility on competitive pricing. The result will be more profits, more staying power, and more pricing flexibility for both the spun-off business unit and for us. Within our vertical markets, we will maintain exclusive distribution rights to the products, so there is no downside from a competitive standpoint."

Mary Anne spoke with a positive yet forceful tone. "Look, we are not going to get caught like we did seven years ago where our PC product prices went below our cost to produce them, let alone distribute them. It's too easy to get caught in that trap. Hugh, I'm sorry. I can't let that happen to this company."

Hugh reclined in his chair as he combed his fingers through his silver hair, a habit he acquired years earlier that indicated to everyone he was thinking about something pretty heavily. "I understand Mary Anne, and it is making more sense to me, but one more thing: What about our worldwide sales and distribution systems? By spinning off the business units, won't this limit what worldwide sales and distribution can sell?"

Confidently and with undaunted assurance, Mary Anne continued. "Good point, Hugh. Interestingly, this move actually frees up our sales channel to look for other products that are possibly more competitive and a better fit for our markets. By breaking the business units off independently, we can focus our thinking on getting the best products through our true core, our distribution and world wide sales and support channels, rather than using our resources to defend our current product line and the future of the business units. And frankly Hugh, the spinout would allow the business units to really go after optimizing their processes and costs, making them much healthier than if they remained inside the company."

"Good point, Mary Anne, continue." She knew that she had won Hugh over. The rest of the resistance would soon follow.

"We will retain an ownership stake in the business units to maintain our exclusive distribution of their products for our markets. This will allow them to distribute the product through other companies who cover other markets not interfering with our own. Additionally, by maintaining the follow-on product development rights, we can do what we do best: additions and modifications to improve the quality and features of the products when the time comes. We need to spin them off now, at the height of their maturity, not protect them as a part of the company anymore. If we hang on to them any longer, it will hinder us from putting the next generation products through our worldwide sales and distribution systems, thus placing us behind the competition and securing our position as a maturing corporation. Additionally, by keeping the business units inside the company, we forfeit the strategic and financial benefits of the product being sold in other markets that we don't even cover, and more importantly, don't have any desire or strategic intent to cover. Let's be realistic gentlemen, five years from now, as we have evidence of already, our main revenues will be coming from new businesses, not our current business units. It is time we free them from our corporate embrace, for our financial and strategic success." Mary Anne felt content with her answer and so did Hugh.

"Mary Anne, this is a completely different structure you know. It defies industry standards, everything we have ever known to be true for a technology company. Everyone is going to think we are crazy. How will the stockholders react?"

Hugh sat back in his chair and listened as the chairman and CEO spoke her familiar analogy: "Gentlemen, we are no longer a manufacturing industry, rather a creative industry. Look at what happened to the film industry of the past—antitrust, technological changes and the entrance of television caused serious repercussions and effects on the way films were made, bought, and distributed. Our industry is no exception. Our products, yes they differ from film but our structure must be conducive to the same kind of creative process as a film, publishing, or any other creative industry company. Yes Hugh, to survive we must defy industry standards, but to succeed as no one before us has done, we must do it better than anyone else."

She sat her coffee mug down on the glass topped cherry table and stared squarely into the monitor, unflinching. They knew she was right.

The fiery redheaded CEO continued as she removed her blazer and hung it delicately on the back of the chair: "The second step I propose is to spin the research lab off, independently, as a privately run organization."

"Mary Anne," Mark Sayberg interrupted this time, "I have a real problem with this one."

Mary Anne had anticipated his opposition, down to the very last second. She noticed how his glasses sat snugly on his large nose and his disheveled hair had grown gray over the years with age: he wouldn't be so easy to win over. Mark Sayberg was a former Industrial Research Institute Chairman and Research and Development Lab manager. He had written countless books on the importance of corporate Research and Development over the past 20 years, and now he was a University Professor at MIT. His resistance was prepared for and Mary Anne paused graciously as he took full advantage of her invitation to interrupt.

"Granted, you turned the lab around six years ago from something we tossed money at to show off our inventions that never materialized into anything other than show-and-tell, and made it into something useful to the company and to the products we sell. You developed a method for spinning out 'single-product' companies instead of projects. It really closed the gap between what we were doing in R&D and what we were selling through our distribution channels. It was pure genius. But didn't we just win the President's award for advanced research? The lab is doing an outstanding job at fueling our distribution channels with new-to-the-world products. The lab spun off 45 companies in the past three years alone. Do you seriously want to give it all up, give it away to private owners?"

"Yes," Mary Anne replied with boldness, "I do. Mark, I agree with what you said completely. You are absolutely right. Our lab is a national treasure, one of the top three labs of its kind in the world. That is exactly why we need to give it a free charter to focus all research and energy into the development of new companies that will become the future of technology. A charter that is without our bias and interference."

Mark stopped her again and sighed. "Mary Anne, how do we know that our lab would survive? It would be a great disservice to humanity to kill it like that. It has contributed more to the current paradigm of technology and computing than any other research lab in the world. Without it, we would not be having this virtual meeting right now."

Mary Anne smiled and, once again, agreed. "Mark, you are correct in every way. The lab can sustain itself based on two things: private and government contracts and investments based on the spinouts' successes. The investment results from liquidating their spinouts will be sufficient to sustain the lab after the first five to seven years. Until that time, government and private contracting will be necessary for the continuation of the lab. There is no reason that a corporation such as ours has to support the Research and Development lab out of our overhead expenditures."

The statement was firm and challenged Mark and the other directors point blank. Mary Anne continued without hesitation, "Additionally gentlemen, part of my proposal is to name the lab after the founder of the company, so that as the lab continues its unprecedented success, our corporation will always be associated with that success."

Kevin Melbourne, an entrepreneur in his late fifties who owned a significant share of the company due to a merger done in a few years ago, came to Mary Anne's defense.

"Mark," he began as his Australian origin seeped through his otherwise British accent, "I took the liberty of calling the Chairman of Sarnoff today, formerly RCA's research lab turned private."

"Yes, Kevin, I am familiar with it." Mark added coolly.

"Based on my interview with him," Kevin continued, "I completely agree with Mary Anne's decision. This is truly the way to go in this matter"

Mary Anne leaned back in her chair and thought *what a delightful surprise, I may have just won this one.*

Mark, with the assistance of Kevin, allowed logic and reason to influence his biased opinion on the matter, and he agreed, despite his emotional reservations.

"I believe we need to vote on these issues now, gentlemen." Mary Anne added as she motioned for the Secretary of the Board.

Timothy put the issue up to vote. "I need a motion to approve this recommendation."

Martin Gregory, her confidant and former venture capitalist, was the first to speak: "Ms. Chairman, I motion to approve."

Kevin Melbourne seconded the motion, and surprisingly, Mark seconded the motion as well. With a unanimous vote in favor, Chairman and CEO Mary Anne Porter relaxed into her chair with utter relief.

"The next item on the agenda," as Timothy Bryant continued, "Ms. Chairman, would you like to introduce it?"

"Yes, Timothy. Gentleman, I would like to introduce you to our new focus, the best products that will feed our distribution systems and will fuel our future on the technological forefront. No decisions need to be made today, but I must rely on your excellent judgement and diverse management experiences in determining which companies we will take a minority stake in to service our worldwide markets. Before I introduce the first startups, I want to congratulate you on making the most important decisions that this company has ever faced. You have chartered the right for the company to succeed. Let it not be said that anyone here inhibited the realization of that success. Now, allow me to introduce the startups…"

Chapter 1

Losing the Leadership: How the Information Technology Leaders of the 1980's Lost their Leadership by 2001

How can large technology companies with the resources, money, power, global reach, talent, patent portfolios, brands, production capacities, and market leadership positions that Lucent, Xerox, IBM and others enjoyed lose out to new companies starting with almost nothing and very little capital? It seems impossible. Yet it did happen and is continuing to happen. In the 1980's and 1990's, every leading computer company lost out to startups created during that era. By 2001, IBM was the only company of the computer market leaders in the 1980's that was still in the general purpose computing business, and even IBM's worldwide market share had dropped from a dominant 66% in 1975 to a mere 17% by 1992[1]. The market share winners were startups created in the 1970's and 1980's who often were able to use the leader's own technology to beat them. In the late 1990's and beginning 2000's, a very similar scenario is being played out in the communications industry (more on that in Chapter 7).

I call this pattern the "Slingshot Syndrome." The syndrome appears to be particularly successful when the markets involved are being disrupted by rapid technological change, putting a premium on rapid commercialization of new technology. The term is derived from the biblical story of David and Goliath where David slayed the arrogant, heavily armored and unsuspecting giant with a mere slingshot, and then decapitated Goliath with the giant's own sword. The startups with their slingshots of new-to-the-world products and rapid commercialization are going to battle with the Goliaths of the information technology industry—and are winning. How is this possible?

One is tempted to blame bad management of the losing giant companies for their troubles, and a number of authors have written analyses along that line; however the facts strongly indicate a much more systemic set of problems that are apparently faced by all. But are they inescapable?

Why did each of these companies, especially the ones who held the future technologies and paradigms in the palm of their hand, not get to the future first? **The answer in each case is that they were distracted by the need to protect their current businesses, product lines, revenue streams, profit streams, personnel, and manufacturing facilities. They were so distracted with the present that they lost sight of the future, and in many cases, they destroyed their own future with the discontinuation of projects that would become the next generation technologies. These new technologies and paradigms were threatening their existing sources of revenue and profits, so the corporation moved to protect them rather**

1 International Data Corporation, 1993.

than invest in what was threatening them. In doing so, they were unable to invest in their own future.

Let me tell you an illustrative story. In 1981, as a young Member of Technical Staff at AT&T's Bell Labs, I was given the assignment to predict the future of distributed computing, and to propose a strategy for the Bell Labs Computing and Networking Technology Department that I was later to head. I had the good fortune of receiving an invitation to visit Xerox's Palo Alto Research Lab, known as PARC, where I was shown their experimental Alto workstations networked together with their experimental Ethernet. The Alto workstation had icons, overlapping windows, drag-and-drop, a WYSIWYG ("What You See Is What You Get") text editor (similar to the current Microsoft Word), a bit-mapped screen, pop-up menus, was controlled by a mouse, and was networked over Ethernet to print servers running laser printers.

This may all seem very familiar and quite obvious today, but at that time, IBM had just introduced the PC, which included one floppy drive, 18 *kilobytes* of memory, no hard drive, and no mouse. A 32-employee company named Microsoft had just introduced MS-DOS. The Apple Macintosh was still three years in the future, and computer terminals and PC's had command-style (think of MS DOS) interfaces and were connected to mainframes or minicomputers with telephone wires running 300 to 1200 bits per second. Printers were still of the impact printing variety, either slow desktops that were essentially modified electric typewriters or large, faster, noisy chain or drum printers in computer rooms.

Bell Labs' computing environment, which was state-of-the-art, consisted of IBM, Amdahl, Univac, and Honeywell mainframes, a Cray supercomputer, and scores of Digital Equipment Corporation minicomputers hooked to "dumb" terminals over telephone lines.

This may sound like a lot of technical gibberish, but what I saw at PARC was a glimpse of the future that became the computing paradigm of today and now runs in our offices and homes. When the PARC innovations were later combined with the PC and the Internet, it changed the world and created the modern information age.

I was very impressed with what I saw, so impressed in fact, that I went back to Bell Labs to write a memorandum informing my supervisors that Xerox had invented the future of computing and all computing would be organized that way in the future. I further proposed that AT&T (the then owner of what is now Lucent and Bell Labs) should partner closely with Xerox since it was clear to me that Xerox was in a position to take over the computer industry from the companies that currently reigned: IBM, Digital Equipment (now part of Compaq), Univac (now part of Unisys), Control Data Corporation, Honeywell, Burroughs (now part of Unisys), Wang, Data General, and NCR. Finally, I proposed that Bell Labs should be wired with Ethernet immediately, in an effort to deploy this new form of computing as soon as possible as well as understand the implications on communications technology.

At that time, AT&T's Western Electric (later renamed Lucent) communications products were completely dominated by circuit switching technology rather than the packet switching technology that Ethernet and the Internet were beginning to demonstrate, although Bell Labs and Western Electric's internal computer network was already running a early version of TCP/IP, the packet switching protocol that later powered the Internet.

I included in my recommendation a request for sufficient budget to cover the expenses for a Bell Labs–wide Intranet. The number was large enough and the plan was grand enough to require the approval of a Vice President. That was my first personal experience with a Bell Labs Vice President. I recall him carefully examining the samples of Ethernet coaxial cable that I brought along, as well as the "fang" connector. He then told me that I had the right idea, and that he would approve the large budget I was requesting! But I would have to do it with Bell Labs technology, not anything developed by Xerox, and he sent me to scour the research department for a competitive technology. I did just that and discovered that within Bell Labs Research, a promising version of packet switching was being developed that was later to be called "cell switching." Cell switching, which involved switching short, fixed-length packets, appeared to have a number of advantages over both circuit switching and the versions of packet switching being used in Ethernet and elsewhere. I worked with the researchers and developers to build enough prototypes of their switch (called Datakit) to serve the 20,000 computer terminals in Bell Labs. We interconnected the cell switches with light fibers, making it the first cell-switched light fiber packet network in operation in the world. A cell-switched packet network connected by light fiber is the telecommunications industry's current (2001) view of the future and Bell Labs had it running internally in 1986.

By 1986 (the same year a small startup named Cisco shipped its first product), I had overseen the deployment within Bell Labs of not only the largest operational cell-switched fiber data network on earth, but also the first intranet, protected by the first firewall (invented in Bell Labs Research), and the first large corporate single-directory email system. Bell Labs' and Western Electric's (later to be renamed Lucent) backbone corporate network (named BLN or the Bell Labs Network) was a packet switched design based on an early version of TCP/IP (which when introduced by DARPA[2] into the public domain in 1982 created the Internet) and had been operational in Bell Labs since 1979. I know this to be a fact because I authored the BLN Internet Protocol (IP) and Transaction Control Protocol (TCP) modules myself, as well as led the BLN project through its first release.

I had been inspired by a presentation given by Vint Cerf (who deserves the title of "the father of the Internet") at a data communications conference at Snowbird, Utah in 1977, where he described TCP and IP standards that he and others were working on. I went back to Bell Labs and

---

2 The US Defense Department's Advanced Research Project Agency

coded it into BLN, and had it running as a production network in 1979, 3 years before the TCP/IP standard was released into the public domain by the Defense Advanced Research Project Agency (DARPA). Note that BLN was routing IP-like packets around Western Electric and Bell Labs 7 years before Cisco released their first router. By 1986 the BLN and Datakit prototype networks were the backbone networks of Bell Labs and Western Electric, interconnecting two continents via the first undersea light fiber cable, linking over 20,000 nodes and 28 locations, and carrying a very heavy traffic load every day.

Because the Internet then was still a very open community of researchers, the Bell Labs Network (BLN) in the latter 1980's actually was carrying much of the bulletin board and email backbone traffic of the Internet. AT&T converted the cell switching prototypes that we had deployed in Bell Labs into two data switching product lines (Datakit VCS and ISN), converted the Bell Labs email system (POST) into the AT&Tmail email service, and merged some of the prototype networking features into its Unix and Computer Systems products, but the BLN itself was never commercialized.

Two other pieces of the puzzle of what became the modern computer paradigm also came from Bell Labs in this time frame: the UNIX operating system and the C (as well as the later C++) programming language. UNIX was the operating system of choice for the Internet developers, with the effect that to this day, servers running the UNIX operating system handle the majority of web traffic. The C and C++ programming languages came to dominate to an even larger extent. By the early 1990's, almost everything related to communications systems, the Internet, and PC's was written in either C or C++, replacing the dozens of programming languages that had preceded them. The Java programming language, which caused a great stir when it was introduced in the mid-1990's, was nothing more than a clever derivation of Bell Labs' C++ programming language. The dominance achieved by UNIX and C were so great that the leading computer companies formed the Open Systems Foundation (OSF) consortium in the late

1980's to leverage their combined strength in order to prevent AT&T from monopolizing the future computing paradigm!

As a result of these events, by the early to mid 1980's Xerox and Bell Labs had every technology they needed to become the dominant forces in the new computing and networking paradigm that was to unfold, and were running them in prototype form inside of their research labs. Despite the fact that both companies did succeed at turning some of their internal prototypes into products, they lost the leadership almost immediately to new startups. The Apple Macintosh, introduced in 1984, took the Xerox Alto workstation concepts and made them affordable to consumers, something Xerox never did. In 1979, 3Com was founded to commercialize Ethernet. In 1982, SUN Microsystems was founded and merged the Alto workstation concept with UNIX, the Motorola 68000 microprocessor, and DARPA's TCP/IP Internet protocols to commercialize the concept of a professional workstation. In 1984, H-P formed an internal startup to commercialize laser printers. Finally, in 1985 Microsoft commercialized the Alto iconic interface into their first release of Windows, which transformed it from a mediocre software company to the dominant player it is today.

Meanwhile, Xerox chose to focus its resources on its survival in the copier business, where it faced competitive attack from Japanese manufactures. Lucent (then part of AT&T) focused its R&D resources on the digital circuit switching of voice communications in order to protect its Electronic Switching Systems business from competitive threats from Nortel, ITT (now Alcatel) and Ericson. Both succeeded at fending off the attackers to their core businesses, although not without loss of market share and loss of access to the new developing markets.

By 2001, Lucent was telling its customers that packet switching is the future of all communications, replacing circuit switching. In Lucent's 2000 Annual Report, a year in which the Lucent stock fell from $82 to $18 per share and the Chairman and CEO was fired by the board of directors, Lucent noted that "lower revenues in switching products primarily due to the shift in customers away from circuit switching ... negatively impacted growth."[3] In the same report Henry Schacht, Lucent's Chairman and CEO, said that Lucent would "fully focus [the] business on delivering the next-generation Internet."[4] By 2001, Lucent admitted that it was for sale and was fighting off rumors of impending bankruptcy after losing $3.7 billion in the first quarter of that year. Standard & Poor's cut Lucent's once stellar debt rating to that of junk bonds (BB-plus)[5] in the middle of 2001, while Xerox bonds were cut to a junk rating in 2000. Xerox was also fighting rumors of impending bankruptcy,[6] having fired its CEO in May 2000 and losing $292 million in 2000[7] and $289 million in the first three-quarters of 2001.[8] Despite these events, the startups created from Lucent and Xerox's inventions had developed a total market value of around 1 trillion dollars! If Xerox had managed to maintain as little as 1% ownership in each of the companies formed around its inventions, it would have more than four times its 2001 market capitalization! Cisco, the company that was founded in 1986 to commercialize network technology similar to what Bell Labs had been running internally since 1979, briefly became the most valuable company on earth in 2000, surpassing both Lucent's and AT&T's valuations.

Lucent and Xerox were not alone in this bloodbath—Palo Alto Research Center's (PARC) historic breakthroughs were known during this period to the technical community within other large information technology companies as well. The computer industry leaders in the early 1980's consisted of IBM, Univac, Burroughs, Honeywell, Digital Equipment, Wang, Data General, Amdahl, NCR, AT&T, Prime, Perkin Elmer, Gould, Cray and

---

3 Lucent Technologies, *2000 Annual Report*, pg. 17.

4 Lucent Technologies, "Chairman's Message", *2000 Annual Report*.

5 Reuter's, June 12, 2001.

6 *Business Week*, March 5, 2001.

7 Xerox Corporation, *2000 10-K Report, as amended in June 27, 2001.*

8 Xerox Corporation, "Third Quarter Results," www.xerox.com, October 23, 2001.

Control Data. None of these companies moved into a leadership role in commercializing the Xerox breakthroughs either, although Digital deserves an honorable mention for playing a significant role in the Ethernet commercialization. Instead, they left the field wide-open to new startups such as SUN, Apollo (later bought by Hewlett Packard), 3Com, Cisco, Apple, and then Dell, Compaq, and Microsoft to introduce these breakthrough technologies into the market. Note that of the industry leaders of early to mid 1980's, only IBM remains as an independent general purpose computer manufacturer 15 years later. Univac and Burroughs merged into Unisys, Digital Equipment was bought by one of the startups (Compaq), and Honeywell sold its computer operation to the French company Group Bull. Wang, Data General, Cray, and Control Data are either no longer in the general-purpose computer hardware business or no longer exist. NCR is still in the computer business, but only with special purpose data warehouse machines known as Teradata.

Why was IBM the exception to this almost complete turnover of computer manufacturers? One answer is that IBM did something in the early 1980's that none of its competitors did. It was a move that IBM had never done before, nor has done since. IBM created within their corporate walls a startup operation that was so removed from the usual IBM controls and culture that it was kept a secret from the other IBM divisions. They basically hid the entire project in order to give it the nimbleness required to create a new market without any interference from their existing business units or functions. That startup was the PC division, located in Boca Raton, Florida, miles from any other IBM presence. The removal of the PC division from the controls of the corporate environment certainly contributed to its enormous success; its open architecture was of equal significance to the modern information industry as the Xerox PARC inventions, the Internet, or the Bell Labs contributions.

IBM would probably still be the leading PC manufacturer in the world if it had not attempted to fold the PC division back into the company, rather than leaving it to operate as an independent startup with its own culture and controls. What happened was that in the early 1990's IBM's most profitable product line, the mainframe computers, came under severe attack, threatening the viability of the whole company. IBM's attention was diverted to that issue and what to do about it. While its attention was diverted, the 1980's startups Compaq and Dell gained market share and eventually passed IBM as market share leaders in the mid-1990's. By 2001, Dell, a company that started operating in a dorm room in 1984, was the largest PC maker on earth and rumors were spreading that IBM may exit the PC business after a number of unprofitable years and sagging sales.

In the communications equipment business, things played out differently, but no better for the entrenched companies. In 1984, AT&T settled the government antitrust suit that had been filed in 1969 by breaking itself up into the Regional Bell Operating Companies (RBOCs) and retaining only the long distance company and the equipment manufacturing company (Western Electric) and R&D (Bell Labs). The Regional Bell Operating Companies for the first time were completely free to buy their equipment from any company. They immediately started courting ITT, GTE, Nortel, Ericson, and Siemens.

The split-up of AT&T came at the worst possible moment for Western Electric, because telephone switching was just starting to convert from analog to digital switches, and Western Electric was behind. AT&T responded to this threat by handing Bell Labs a virtual blank check to do whatever it took to build the best digital switch in the world, and to do it fast. With so much at stake to protect its existing equipment business, AT&T, Bell Labs, and Western Electric had no time to pay any attention to new computer paradigms from Xerox's PARC, the emerging packet switching protocols from DARPA, cellular communications which it had co-invented with Motorola, or the new cell-switching technologies from its own research lab. The resulting digital switch, the 5ESS, was the largest project ever undertaken by Bell Labs, eclipsing its earlier work on the Anti Ballistic Missile system (SAFEGUARD), Bell Labs contribution to

NASA's Apollo Program moon shot, or PicturePhone. But it was a success, and by the late 1980's two of 5ESS's competitors had exited (ITT and GTE), Ericson and Siemens had decided to compete in other markets, leaving only Nortel as a serious competitor in the United States.

In the 1970's, like Xerox, AT&T together with its Bell Labs and Western Electric subsidiaries had actually developed what turned out to be a very good vision of the future Internet services. They foresaw a world in which intelligent services would appear to be inside of the network, and customers would be able to access these services without knowledge of where the computers were physically located. They attempted to implement such a network and called it ACS and later NET1000. One of the first services was to be travel services. The technology chosen to make it work was not suitable or ready, and AT&T gave up in the early 1980's after spending more than $1 billion.

One of the reasons that AT&T invested in NET1000 to begin with was the purchase by IBM of Satellite Business Systems, a satellite carrier that allowed corporate customers to bypass AT&T's long distance telephone network. AT&T was afraid that IBM would create a data communications infrastructure that had no need for AT&T's telephone network. So AT&T countered by attempting to create a computing service that had no need for the customers to buy IBM's mainframes. The same year that AT&T announced that it was discontinuing NET1000, IBM sold SBS to MCI. Presumably, both companies thought that their nightmares were over once the other had ceded incursion into each other's market spaces. What both of them missed was that the nightmare was real—there would be a bypass intelligent data network that would make owning mainframe computers superfluous. It would be called the Internet, and it would be built by hundreds of companies that IBM and AT&T had never heard of or who did not exist at the time. It would, just like they both worried, challenge both of their leadership positions in computer manufacturing and communications.

In 1995, in anticipation of the effects of the US Telecommunications Act of 1996, AT&T CEO Bob Allen decided to break up AT&T once again, splitting equipment manufacturing (Lucent and NCR) from the long distance operations (AT&T). A result was that Bell Labs stayed with Lucent. An unexpected side effect of the Telecommunications Act of 1996 was that it created a huge, but temporary demand for telecommunications equipment. The Regional Bell Operating Companies, suddenly aware that they would soon face competition in the local services monopolies from many sides (AT&T, Cable Companies, and new Competitive Local Exchange Carriers), decided *en masse* that they should use their monopoly revenues, while they still had them, to upgrade their antiquated networks to meet the certain competition.

Since most of their installed equipment was either made by Lucent or Nortel, this created an enormous boom for both companies just as Lucent was set free from AT&T. Although the Internet age as we know it now was created in 1994 by the introduction of the first browser and the allowance by the US government of commercial activity on "the net," Lucent was far too busy meeting the demand for voice network upgrades from Regional Bell Operating Companies to notice or think about it. Instead of taking advantage of its leadership and understanding of packet switching, cell switching and optical interconnects that it had been building up internally for over a decade, Lucent let a new raft of startups take the lead in all three categories because it were too busy with temporary demand.

By the end of the 1990's, having realized its mistake, Lucent feverishly used its highly inflated stock to buy up startups in these categories, and used its excellent bond ratings to buy market share with the Competitive Local Exchange Carriers (CLEC's) by advancing them more than enough credit to buy their equipment. But it was too little, too late: in 2000, as the Regional Bell Operating Companies (RBOC's) decided that their network upgrades were completed, Lucent stock fell from $81 per share at the end of 1999 to $5 per share in 2001. The Lucent CEO was fired, and serious enough liquidity problems surfaced that the bond rating was cut to junk. By early 2001, rumors of liquidity problems and potential bankruptcy surfaced, and Lucent was attempting to sell off enough assets to remain a going concern. By the spring of 2001, the CFO had been fired and it was clear that Lucent as a whole was for sale, if they could find an interested buyer. When Lucent's fiscal year closed at the end of September, 2001, they reported a mind-numbing loss of $16 billion ($11 billion of which was due to restructuring charges and other one-time charges).

If Nortel was faring better, it could not be determined from the financial reports. Both companies announced layoffs and divestitures that essentially cut their total number of employees in half during 2001 alone. Nortel blew almost everyone's mind by reporting a $22 billion net loss in the first half of 2001 ($14 billion of which were due to write-downs of acquisitions and inventory), which helped bring its stock price down 94% to under $5 from its previous year high of over $82. The possibility that the new generation of communications equipment startups, ranging from optical switching to cell switching to soft switching technology, would grab the market lead from the likes of Lucent and Nortel had become a virtual certainty.

Chapter 2

Capital Markets: the Polarization of
Patient and Impatient Money

One of the reasons that we have traditionally thought that entrenched competitors have an automatic advantage to getting to the future first, ahead of startup companies, is their access to capital. Between their retained earnings, ability to float stock offerings, access to the corporate bond market, and preferential treatment by banks, they have traditionally enjoyed a huge and often insurmountable advantage over a startup. But as of the 1980's, this all started to change.

One of the changes born in the 1980's, and strengthened in the 1990's, was the *shareholder rights* movement and its effect on corporate governance. Before 1980, large American corporations were run by the hired managers who had little to fear from their shareholders or the share-holder's representatives—the board of directors. The result was the economic stagnation of the 1970s, as American companies were overtaken by their overseas competitors in everything from profitability to innovation to quality. The corporate management was running the company for the good of management and the employees, rather than the owners. This started to change around 1980 when financiers such as Henry Kravis, Carl Icahn and T. Boon Pickens discovered that one could take over a public company using borrowed money, and then greatly increase its financial performance by replacing the management and tying the new management to strict annual and quarterly financial goals.

The 1980's became known as the age of the corporate raider and the leveraged buy-out (LBO). So successful were the returns, that between 1984 and 1990, net new issues of equity were negative, meaning that more stock was being privatized via LBOs than was being issued by new and existing companies.[9]

The corporate raiders had an amazing effect on US business. It has been estimated that 57% of large US firms were either takeover targets or were restructured on their own as a result of the takeover threat.[10] Using leveraged buyouts as the vehicle, the capital markets essentially took over control of the priorities of the corporation from the corporate managers, and re-oriented them toward the shareholders. The new owners of bought-out corporations put in place managers who were loyal to the owners rather than the corporation. The new management teams cut the excess capacity that had built up under the previous management, significantly increasing corporate profits.[11]

---

9 Kaplan, Steven N. "The Evolution of U.S. Corporate Governance: We are all Henry Kravis Now." *Conference on the Power and Influence of Pension and Mutual Funds*, New York, February 21, 1997.

10 Mitchell, M. and Hulherin, H. "The Impact of Industry Shocks on Takeover and Restructuring Activity." *Journal of Financial Economics* (1996), pp. 193-229.

11 Poterba, James, Working Paper, MIT (1997).

The increase in financial performance was so dramatic using this "Leveraged Buy-out" (LBO) approach that institutional stockholders, who in their indexed portfolios had no option but to own shares in many of the largest American corporations, decided to force the same financial discipline onto their investments that the LBO funds were forcing. CalPERS, the California Public Employees Retirement System and the largest US pension fund, was particularly active in using its shareholdings for this purpose. If a CEO did not meet the quarterly or annual goals set by the board of directors, he (and it almost always was a he) was fired and replaced with someone who could. In the early 1990's, the names of companies who had their CEOs ousted by their own boards read like a Who's Who of the large American corporations at the time: American Express, Chrysler, General Motors, IBM, Kodak, and Westinghouse. By the end of the 1990's AT&T, Lucent and Xerox had also joined that club. All had their CEOs replaced by the board for financial under-performance. For all CEOs, the message was clear: meet the board's and the market's expectations, or your career is over. Simultaneously, the boards increased the incentive compensation for CEOs dramatically, making the best CEOs fabulously well paid.

Institutional investors, particularly CalPERS, Robert Monks' and Nell Minow's LENS Investment Management, and Michael Price's Mutual Shares funds, became particularly aggressive in what was billed as a "boardroom revolution" led by "shareholder's rights advocates."[12] Shareholder's rights was a movement started in 1986 by T. Boone Pickens when he formed the United Shareholder's Association (USA) as a non-profit advocacy group for shareholder's rights. The group operated until 1993, when it was disbanded because it had come to the conclusion that its objectives had been achieved. Indeed they had—in 1992, the SEC relaxed a key rule making it much easier for shareholders to coordinate challenges to under-performing management teams. Before 1992, the SEC required shareholders to file detailed proxy statements with the SEC before being allowed to communicate with other shareholders. The new rules made it possible for shareholders to talk at any time, provided that they send a summary of the discussion to the SEC after the fact. CalPERS and USA, among others, lobbied hard with the SEC for the rule change. The Business Roundtable and other management organizations argued very strongly against it, presumably because their members foresaw the radical change it would have on how corporations are governed.

Other regulatory changes played a role as well. In 1988, the US Department of Labor (DOL) issued a letter that warned pension plan trustees that their voting rights had to be exercised with diligence as one aspect of their fiduciary duties. Pension funds such as CalPERS interpreted this letter (acknowledging the courts traditionally refer to DOL publications for guidance on fiduciary duty) as instructions that they could no longer play a passive investment role, even though their funds were primarily index funds as opposed to actively managed funds. In order to track an index such as the Wilshire 2500, CalPERS must own shares of most of the 2500 companies in that index. CalPERS concluded that the main method for improving their investment returns was to use the voting power of their shares to get corporate management teams to take the necessary actions to maximize shareholders' returns. With the 1988 DOL letter, this was not only good financial management practice, but became their fiduciary duty. In 1994, the DOL updated the original letter with language that clearly advocated an activist corporate role for pension plan trustees, including "activities intended to monitor or influence corporate management."[13]

---

12 Ball, David George "Revolution in the Board Room?" St. Johns Law Review (March 1994); Clurman, Richard M. "Who's in Charge?", *Whittle* (1993), Coardiz, Dan "Corporate Hangmen," *Financial World* (March 30, 1993); Lohr, Steve "Pulling Down the Corporate Clubhouse," *The NY Times* (April 12, 1992).

13 *DOL Interp. Bulletin* 94-1 (July 1994).

While pension funds and other institutional stockowners were increasing their shareholder activism to improve their portfolio financial returns, they were also increasing their ownership of US corporations. While institutions owned only 30% of all corporate equity in the United States in 1970, by 1980 it had climbed to 40% and by 1994 54%.[14] Ownership of public equity by institutional investors is even higher, meaning that by the 1990's the institutions were firmly in the driver's seat among shareholders.

Shareholder activism is not confined just to the institutional investors, either. The rise of the internet bulletin boards has added a whole new dimension to shareholders ability to communicate with other shareholders. This has allowed small individual shareholders to band together and get corporate management to listen and act on their concerns and agendas. There are even special web sites oriented toward helping shareholders to become organized. One of them is tellingly named eRaider.com, which includes a mutual fund to invest in targeted under-performing companies. eRaider is not shy about taking legal actions to remove management, asking the SEC to force disclosures, or starting proxy fights for control of their targets. Even CalPERS has started using the Internet to conduct shareholder forums and to post its planned votes on proxy issues.[15]

The effect on American corporations and the American stock market has been dramatic. Restructuring became the theme of business starting in the 1980's, and the stock market rose from a Dow of 800 in 1982 to over 11,000 by 2000, largely driven by the dramatic increase of earnings that ensued. The resulting bull market was the longest in history, and American industry moved back into its postwar position as the most competitive in the world. Governmental deregulation and aggressive antitrust enforcement broke down the monopolies that had reigned technology in

---

14 Poterba, James and Samwick, Andrew *Brookings Papers on Economic Activity* (1996).

15 Steindorf, Sarah "A Place at the Table," *Christian Science Monitor* (November 11, 2000)

the previous decades: AT&T, IBM, Xerox, Polaroid were all subjected to serious competition for the first time in the 1970's. The AT&T and IBM antimonopoly suites filed in 1969 were both settled in the early 1980's with agreements to open up their markets to competition.

Although this produced enormous benefits to the economy, employment, stockholders and consumers, it had an unanticipated side effect. With the 1990's, CEOs completely focused on meeting the financial objectives of the market and the board. They were no longer incented to divert capital into future products and markets. The reason is fairly obvious: future products or markets require years of investing before they result in significant revenue, and even more years before they result in significant profits. On the other hand, current products and services generate all of a corporation's revenue and profits. When a CEO is held closely accountable to quarterly financial results, it only stands to reason that he or she will invest everything into what is generating the revenue and profits at that moment in time. Obviously, they will invest to protect next quarter's or next year's revenues and profits as well. But not next decade's: they will be long gone by then.

This imposition of short-term financial discipline on the large technology firms created a market opportunity for startups. In the same time frame, the traditional access-to-capital problem was solved in the 1980's and 1990's by the venture capital industry. The venture capital industry, which was first established after World War II in an effort to commercialize technologies from MIT, came into its own in the 1980's, and then boomed in the1990's with the commercialization of the Internet. The effect was that startups no longer suffered an access-to-capital disadvantage over the established firms. In fact, when taken together with the effects of the shareholder's rights movement, by the 1990's startups enjoyed an advantage over the established firms in having access to long term or "patient capital." The tables had turned. To understand why this happened, let's have a brief look at how the venture capital industry works.

Venture Capital

Venture capital is almost always organized into 10-year funds that invest in private equity (i.e. non-exchange-traded stock). The funds are raised primarily from pension funds and endowments who allocate a certain percentage of their portfolios to "alternative investments" including venture capital. Because the funds do not abide by SEC regulations meant to protect ordinary investors, they are off limits to most individual investors. But the SEC regards investors of sufficient means, and professional investors, as not needing their protection. So that is where private equity funds, of which venture funds are a large segment, raise their capital.

The purpose of venture capital is to invest in startups with the hope of selling them from 1 year to 10 years later for a substantially higher price. The sale is either a sale to the public on a stock market (IPO), or a private sale to another company (acquisition). Once an investment in a startup has been liquidated via a sale, the fund returns the proceeds to the investor. Most funds attempt to liquidate their entire portfolio within 10 years.

A CEO whose shareholders are venture capitalists is held to a completely different financial discipline than the CEO of a public company. Instead of a focus on profitability in the current quarter, he or she is strongly encouraged to take the right actions to maximize the amount of revenues a few years out. Predictability of financial results is much less important than maximizing the future potential of the company.

Venture capitalists treat their investments quite differently from investors in public companies. For one, they are very actively involved in developing the company. Secondly, they fully expect that as many as half of their investments will not be profitable. They manage their risk by keeping the companies on a short leash, allocating their investments in multiple rounds tied to objective accomplishment, and managing their investment return across their whole portfolio. In a typical venture fund, 60% of the investments lose money for the investors, 20% make 1–2 times return on investment, 10% make 2–5 times return, 7% make 5–10 times return, and

3% make 10 times or higher returns. The mean time between the first round of financing and an IPO is approximately 8 years.[16]

From 1980 to 2000, the amount of capital allocated to venture capital multiplied by a factor of 200, with the biggest increases toward the end of the 1990's. In 1999, total US venture capital raised exceeded $100 billion for the first time, and was nearly double the amount raised in the previous year and five times the amount raised two years earlier. If this rate of increase continues, the total amount of venture capital raised in one year will exceed the annual total R&D expenditures by US industry sometime in the mid first decade of the 21st century, and exceed the total US R&D (including government and university) expenditures a year or two later. Despite the setbacks with Internet investments in 2000, in March of 2001, CalPERS announced that it was increasing its allocation to venture capital by $500M, bringing its total venture capital investment to well over $2 billion.[17]

The effects are that institutional investors, such as CalPERS, have decided that they can obtain a better return for their constituents by, on the one hand, forcing public companies to be accountable to short term financial goals, while on the other hand, financing venture capitalists to develop the new markets, breakthrough products, and breakthrough technologies of the world. This phenomenon first started to happen in earnest in the 1990's and, as the CalPERS 2001 announcement indicates, is very likely to be a permanent change to the US capital market that we will all have to adjust to. The combination of institutionalization of stock ownership, shareholders rights victories, and venture capital alternative investments are reshaping the corporate landscape. The capital markets are making risk capital available to startups and denying it to established companies.

---

16 Data derived from the VentureOne and Thompson Financial's VenturExpert databases.

17 "CalPERS ups the ante in venture capital." *Sacramento Business Journal* (March 26, 2001).

In his 1942 book *Capitalism, Socialism and Democracy*, the economist Joseph Schumpeter wrote: "Capitalism, then, is by nature a form of method of economic change and not only never is, but never will be stationary." Schumpeter continues to add that "The opening of new markets … illustrate the same process of industrial mutation—if I may use that biological term—that incessantly revolutionizes the economic structure *from within*, incessantly destroying the old one, incessantly creating the new one. This process of Creative Destruction is the essential fact about capitalism. It is what capitalism consists in and what every capitalist concern has got to live in." If Peter Schumpeter were alive today, he would be impressed with the degree that the capital markets have institutionalized his principles.

Chapter 3

**Speed of Change: Past and Future Speed
of Change in the Information
Technologies**

The steady, unrelenting fast pace of technological change has two structural effects on the information technology industry: (i) it rapidly undermines the profitability of existing products and manufacturers, and (ii) it creates vast new markets for products and services that are consumers of the processor cycles, memory, and bandwidth that are being created at such a rapid pace. The replacement of old-line stalwarts with new startups is a direct result of the first effect (i), and the dot.com boom is the direct result of the second (ii).

When combined with deregulation and aggressive antitrust, as has been the case in the computer, software, and telecommunications industries in the 1980's and 1990's, these trends have turned stable markets into fast changing markets that tend to favor the startups over the established players. Established corporations will always attempt to shift the balance toward themselves by gaining sufficient market control or enlisting a regulator to slow down the rate of change to a speed they can handle. In the 1960's and 1970's, IBM, Xerox, and Lucent (AT&T) all had such control. But in the 1980's, they lost it. In the 1990's Microsoft and the RBOCs had enough control to be able to slow down the rate of change in their markets, although by the end of the 1990's, they were both in danger of losing market control via further deregulation and antitrust action.

The shift of capital to venture-backed startups would not be nearly as strong, or have the effect that it has, were it not for the incredible speed of change that underlies the information technology industry. If you have worked in information technology, then you may be familiar with *Moore's Law,*[18] named after one of the founders of Intel, which predicted correctly in 1965 the number of transistors that could be placed on one chip would double every year. In 1995 he updated the prediction to once every two years. The effect of Moore's Law is illustrated in Figure 3–1, which shows the decrease in the size of a single memory cell for Dynamic Random Access Memory (DRAM) over a 30 year time period.

18SEE http://www.intel.com/research/silicon/moorespaper.pdf

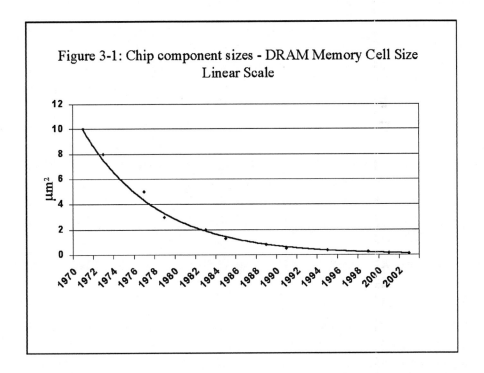

Figure 3-1: Chip component sizes - DRAM Memory Cell Size
Linear Scale

The decrease in memory cell size appears to follow an exponential curve, as the law predicts; however, it is very hard to see exactly what is going on in the tails of an exponential curve because the scales become compressed. By changing one of the scales on the graph to logarithmic, the exponential curve becomes a straight line, as Figure 3–2 illustrates. As one can see, this makes it easy to predict what will happen in the future. This incredible speed of change has held amazingly steady for the last 25 years and shows no signs of abating within the next 5 to 10 years.

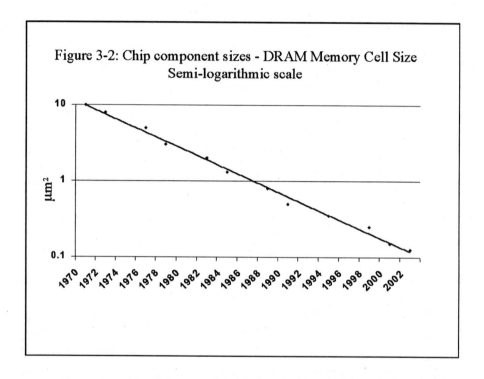

Figure 3-2: Chip component sizes - DRAM Memory Cell Size
Semi-logarithmic scale

The same unrelenting forward march of chip technology that accounts for the reduction of memory cell sizes and hence the increase of memory density effects all other semiconductor circuits as well. It is simply easiest to illustrate with DRAM, since the basic electronic circuit for a DRAM memory cell has not changed in over 30 years. For example, the effect of Moore's Law on microprocessors is that for a given price, the processor power has been doubling roughly every 12 months. Figure 3–3 illustrates this example.

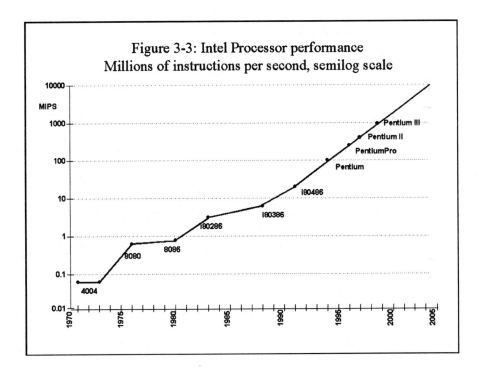

Figure 3-3: Intel Processor performance
Millions of instructions per second, semilog scale

The other way of viewing this is that the cost of producing processors of the same power drops by half every 12 months while the cost of memory drops by half every 2 to 2.5 years. The result of this rapid decrease in costs has been the democratization of computing. The PCs of today, affordable by an ever increasing segment of the world's population, are as powerful as the million dollar behemoths of only a few years ago. This has allowed the information technology industry to grow phenomenally, becoming one of the most important components of economic growth in many countries. It also made possible the unusually strong productivity gains coupled with low inflation that the 1990's saw. These graphs show that the phenomenon will continue for the next 5 to 10 years unabated.

Processor speed and computer memory are not the only rapidly changing technologies. Bandwidth available to residential users and corporations for long-distance networks is now doubling at an even faster pace—every 11 months—as shown in Figure 3–4. Note that in Figure 3–4, the slope of the rate of change shifted abruptly in 1996 through 2001 from the rate it had been experiencing from 1970 through 1995. Interestingly, 1996 is the year that the US Congress passed into law The Telecommunications Act of 1996, which, for the first time in history, opened up local telephone service to competition. The question going forward is whether the rate of change will stay at the new rate, or revert back to the previous rate. Figure 3–4 shows both scenarios. It also compares residential access bandwidth with the bandwidths necessary for compact disk quality sound, HDTV transmission, etc. As can be seen, the new bandwidths offer potential for yet-undreamed-of information services beyond the Internet, television, music and telephone services we are familiar with today.

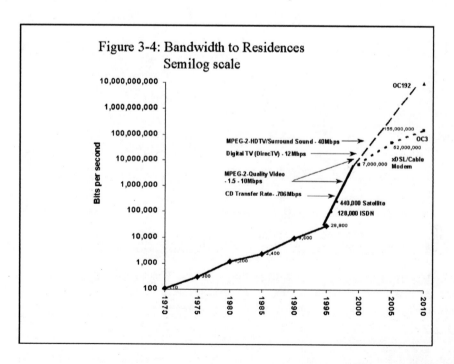

One of the most powerful forces underlying the communications revolution is optical fiber technology. The bandwidth of optical transmission devices is also doubling roughly every year, as can be seen in Figure 3–5. Note that in this chart, as in Figure 3–4, the rate of growth changed dramatically in the 1996 timeframe.

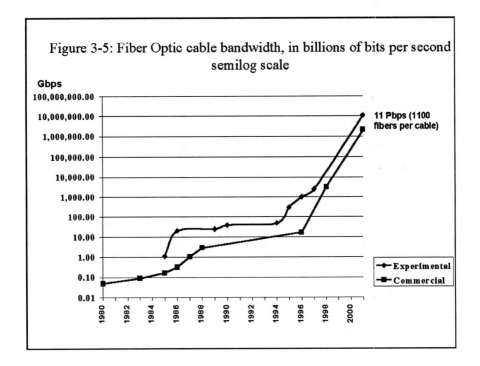

Figure 3-5: Fiber Optic cable bandwidth, in billions of bits per second semilog scale

There are other exponential growth curves underlying the industry. The Internet backbone bandwidth has been doubling every 1.7 years. The cost of wide area data networking is dropping in half every year to 18 months, while the cost of disk storage is dropping in half every 1.8 years. Magnetic disk capacity is doubling every 2.3 years, optical disk capacity every 2.5 years. Compression algorithms are doubling in effectiveness every 3 years. Figure 3–6 compares the rates of change of the two most important information technologies, and illustrates the compounding effect of the rapid change.

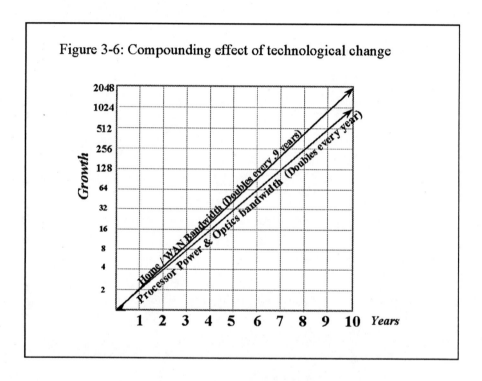

Figure 3-6: Compounding effect of technological change

How new technology gets developed

Where do breakthrough technologies come from? Who develops them? In 1999, the US National Research Council published a comprehensive report on the key information technologies of the previous 35 years.[19] Some of their findings are illustrated in Figures 3–7 and 3–8.

---

19 National Research Council, Computer Science and Telecommunications Board *Funding a Revolution; Government Support for Computing Research.* Washington, DC: National Academy Press (1999).

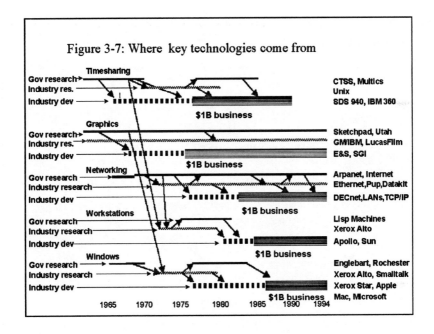

Figure 3-7: Where key technologies come from

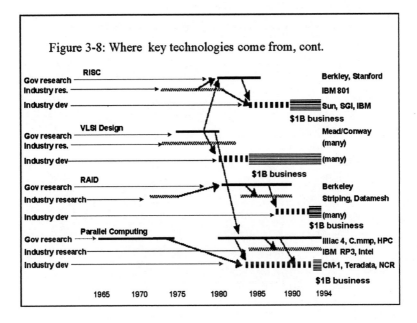

Figure 3-8: Where key technologies come from, cont.

There are a number of interesting observations in Figures 3–7 and 3–8. The most obvious is that key technologies take a surprisingly long time to develop and commercialize. They also go through fits of stops and starts and stops. The effort may start in government labs (which includes universities) and shift to corporate labs, or visa versa. Both types of research labs appear to play key roles. Also, the charts show that the companies that end up leading commercial markets are very often not the companies that did the key research.

It is no wonder that it is so hard for information technology companies to maintain their leads. **Their own technology changes so rapidly that it undermines their market positions.** Their research breakthroughs appear often to benefit their competitors more than themselves. Foster and Kaplan reported in 2001 from their analysis of over 1000 companies over a 36 year period that in the computer hardware, software, and semiconductor industries they found a *negative* correlation between R&D spending and total return to shareholders, meaning that the more a company spent on R&D, the worse their financial performance![20] Clayton Christensen showed how in the disk drive business, industry leadership changed with each new generation of the technology.[21]

Summary

All of the technology trends that disrupted the computer industry in the 1980's and 1990's and allowed the more creative startups to grab the lead are still intact, and will be for the foreseeable future. The amazing rate

---

20 Foster, Richard and Kaplan, Sarah *Creative Destruction: Why Companies that are Built to Last Underperform the Market – and How to Successfully Transform Them.* New York: Currency-Doubleday (2001), pg. 213.

21 Christensen, Clayton M. *The Innovator's Dilemma: When New Technologies Cause Great Firms to Fail.* Boston: Harvard Business School Press (2000).

of cost/performance improvements in silicon will continue. They are now joined by even faster cost/performance improvements in communications technology. The combination of rapidly increasing bandwidth and computer cycles will continue to power the dawning information age, offering huge opportunities to nimble, creative startups and continuing to threaten the survival of the large, entrenched corporation.

Chapter 4

Traditional vs. Startup: Comparing IT Company Structures, Controls, and Systems

What is so different about the venture capital / startup model that makes it more successful at introducing new breakthrough products and services? Can large information technology companies be changed so that they are not forever doomed by the next generation of companies?

The structure of the modern information technology company traces back to 1884, when John Patterson established the National Cash Register Company (NCR). In 1914, Thomas J. Watson, second in command at NCR, left to head C-T-R, which was renamed International Business Machines Corporation in 1924. Although C-T-R was already a manufacturing company when Watson joined it, he brought with him NCR's structure and tactics for sales, support, and distribution.

In the communications industry, Alexander Graham Bell formed the Bell Telephone Company in 1877, which in 1882 acquired the Western Electric Company as its manufacturing arm. Interestingly, Western Electric was founded by Elisha Grey, the same man who lost to Alexander Graham Bell by only a matter of hours in their race to the patent office for the telephone patent in 1876. In 1907, Theodore Vail created the modern structure of AT&T. Among other things, he combined the engineering departments of AT&T with those of Western Electric to create what would be named in 1925 "Bell Laboratories". And in 1995, Lucent was spun off from AT&T, taking the Western Electric manufacturing arm and Bell Labs with it.

In 1945, IBM started IBM Research based on the Bell Labs model of a research lab. In 1970, Xerox founded the Palo Alto Research Lab with a model of industrial research also based heavily on the Bell Labs model. In 1991, Microsoft founded Microsoft Research on a model inspired by Bell Labs.

AT&T, NCR, and IBM were the growth miracles of their day in the latter 19th century and early 20th century. By 1880, Western Electric had already become the largest electrical manufacturing company in the United States, and by 1914, its international locations included Antwerp, London, Berlin, Milan, Paris, Vienna, St. Petersburg, Budapest, Tokyo, Montreal, Buenos Aires, and Sydney. In 1886, NCR was already a multi-national corporation and by 1911 it employed 5900 people in 121 countries. By 1920, IBM had established operations into Asia, Europe, South America, and Australia.

It is easy to see why these three companies set the stage of how all 20th century information technology companies were to be structured. Today, as we enter the 21st century, most information technology companies still retain the structure inherited from these 19'th century giants. That structure consists of an engineering and manufacturing component, a worldwide direct sales component, a worldwide services component, a corporate research organization, and corporate staff departments including Human Resources, Law, Public Relations, Marketing, and Finance. Later variations include organizing the company into business units, where the business units have this structure. Some companies experimented with a "matrix" between the business unit structure and the functional structure, where, for example, a vice president may be the head of worldwide manufacturing but individual plants are "matrixed" into the business units they support, creating a dual reporting structure. In the 1980s and 1990s there was a move to "outsource" some of the functions such as manufacturing, but the structure of the companies still remained the same. See Figure 4–1 for a block diagram view of this structure.

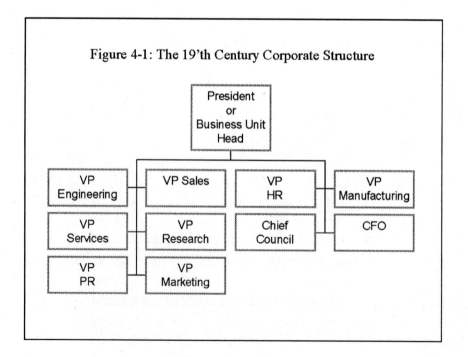

Figure 4-1: The 19'th Century Corporate Structure

The way this type of company works is this: the Marketing department is charged with finding new product markets worldwide. The corporate Research lab is charged with developing new technology. New technology and market needs are combined into business plans. These business plans tell Engineering which new products to develop, and tell Manufacturing which new products to manufacture, and in what volume. As a new product launch approaches, worldwide servicing plans are deployed, including the training of service engineers and deployment of spare parts to all markets. Finally, a worldwide advertising campaign is run with customer events and training programs. All of these are localized to match national cultures and languages.

As the development of a new product advances through this process, there are specific "decision gates" where progress is ascertained, and, if necessary, plans are modified based on problems encountered. At each decision gate, the members of a decision board make a judgment as to whether to proceed with the development, and, if so, whether to allow modifications to the original business plan. The purpose of the decision gates is to assure that the various needed functions (Development, Manufacturing, Supply Line Management, Services, Public Relations, Training, Publishing, etc.) remain coordinated as the product development progresses. Also, it gives the senior management insight into the risks of each project, which they can use to decide which projects to continue, and which to stop.

This model is so successful because it allows quick expansion into international markets, while maintaining the opportunity for tight corporate controls over quality, product lines, inventory, finance, marketing, and personnel. It works particularly well where the development and manufacturing processes are complex, where the markets are stable and well-understood, where worldwide distribution and localization are required, where the business model is well understood, and where there is a relatively low need for innovation. The next release of an existing product fits these qualifications well. But new-to-the world products do not, especially when they involve breakthrough technology, are aimed at poorly understood or new markets, or require a new business model. These types of products are much more likely to succeed in a venture-backed startup. And as the underlying speed of fundamental technological change has accelerated, the advantage has shifted to those companies that can produce the latter type of products, and hence away from the traditional information technology corporation.

Comparison of Approaches

Table 4–1 contrasts how traditionally structured information technology companies manage their business versus venture-backed startups.

Table 4-1
There are fundamental conflicts between the basic management approaches used by large corporations and venture-backed startups

	Corporate	VC/Startup
Compensation	» Primarily Salary » Emphasis on fairness	» Primarily Stock ownership » No concern for fairness
Project Controls	» Decision Gate Processes » Internal Review Boards » Annual Budgets	» Funding Rounds » Board of Directors » Capital Markets
Financial Objectives	» Quarterly P&L Results » Predictable financial results » Stable stock price increases	» Liquidation value of the company within 10 years » >10x return on investment
Staffing / HR	» Internal staff re-use » Career paths, training » Company loyalty	» Hire the appropriate experience / talent » Fire if unproductive

Compensation

The approach for compensation is one area that is treated very differently within a startup than within an established corporation. Compensation in traditional companies is primarily in the form of a predictable salary, with most having some incentive-based compensation for the higher level executives and the sales people. The incentive portion of the total compensation is usually tied to meeting objectives in departmental annual plans plus financial objectives tied to revenue and/or earnings. The corporate Human Resources department builds the compensation plan around a principle of fairness, going to a great deal of trouble to assure that people are compensated fairly based on their backgrounds, education, years of experience, race, ethnicity, gender, accomplishments, responsibility, location, and other factors. In contrast, compensation in a successful venture-backed startup is primarily in the form of stock ownership. If the startup succeeds, compensation can be spectacular, and, if it fails, relatively low. Much emphasis is put on assuring alignment between success from the investor's viewpoint and compensation of the employees. The investors are usually willing to part with a significant amount of ownership in the company to assure that the key employees are motivated along the same lines as they are.

On the other hand, fairness is not a concern. Everyone knows and understands that luck plays a significant role in the degree of success of a startup. One startup team may have the good fortune of hitting the IPO market at just the right moment and be spectacularly rewarded, while another startup team with less fortunate timing is not. This is treated by all as simply part of the game. This radically different approach to compensating key employees has a direct effect on how those employees make decisions. While the leaders and employees of a startup are very highly motivated to maximize the long term capitalization of the company, the leaders and employees of a more established corporation are highly motivated to take the necessary actions to maintain their salaries, benefits, status, and perks. In other words, they are motivated to do what they can to keep their positions, and if possible, rise to a position of higher status, salary, benefits, and perks, even if by doing so they lower capitalization (stock value) of the company. Bonuses based on meeting budget objectives train them in the art of getting large, sometimes inflated budgets approved, thereby assuring that they easily meet or beat their cost objectives. Bonuses tied to revenue objectives motivate them to close deals with poor profitability, or to arrange payments by customers in such a way that revenue moves from bad years to good years. In the bad years they receive no bonus because they cannot meet their targets while, in contrast, in the good years, each additional dollar of revenue raises their compensation. Bonuses tied to profitability cause them to sacrifice projects that will pay off in the future for projects that will pay off in the current year. Stock options, for those who qualify for them, usually do not make up a sufficient portion of the compensation for employees other than the top management to sway their behavior toward maximizing capitalization.

Therefore, it is no wonder that established companies function mostly as bureaucracies, with organizations characterized by specialization of function, adherence to fixed rules, and hierarchy of authority whose primary purpose is self-preservation. Venture-backed startups are primarily motivated to maximize the long-term capitalization of their companies. Since the startup must grow and grow rapidly to meet the goals of its investors, preserving the status quo is unthinkable. Venture capitalists would quickly replace a management team who does not understand this. The effect of these differences in compensation and motivation means that for many decisions, the corporate managers will move in almost exactly the opposite direction as the managers of a venture-backed startup. This will occur in areas varying from spending decisions, employment decisions, project decisions, to what customers to target. The startup manager is motivated to take the lower cost and the riskier bets, while the corporate manager is motivated to take the higher cost and the conservative bets.

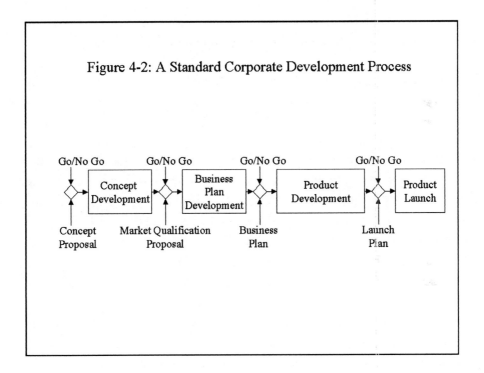

Figure 4-2: A Standard Corporate Development Process

Project Controls

Project controls are different as well. As Figure 4–2 illustrates, traditional information technology companies rely on development processes consisting of a number of discreet decision points where management review boards decide either to proceed or not to proceed with the project. An additional project control tool is the annual budget where decisions are made determining which projects to fund and which to not fund or stop funding. In contrast, project controls in startups consist primarily of venture funding rounds. Between funding rounds, the startups' board of directors interact with the management on a monthly review basis. At each funding round, typically 6 to 12 months apart, the venture capitalists decide whether to continue funding the startup or not. If they decide to not participate in a funding round, the startup CEO is free to find other venture capitalists to fund his/her company. If that fails, the company runs out of money and is shut down. These differences also drive different decision making behavior. The venture-backed startup is more motivated to get the product to market quickly, adapting it as the startup learns the market needs. The corporate project manager is fundamentally motivated to get his or her project through all of the decision points without having it killed. The best way to do that is to pick a conservative project with conservative schedule and cost estimates and no technical or market risk. The engineers on the project are in effect discouraged from being innovative, lest they raise the technical risk and threaten the schedule.

Financial Objectives

The third area of difference is the financial objectives that the management is tied to. To an increasing degree, the CEOs of public corporations are being held to meeting their quarterly earnings projections. Investors reward predictable growth in earnings. Richard Zeckhauser, François Degeorge and Jayendu Patel performed a study of 100,000 quarterly earnings reports from 1974 to 1996 comparing them with analysts' forecasts and found that an unexpectedly large number of the reports exactly matched the analysts' expectations or exceeded them by one cent. Significantly fewer missed analysts' expectations by one cent, indicating that corporations "manage their earnings" to meet or slightly beat analysts' forecasts. Exceeding expectations by very much is not rewarded either, because analysts look for quarter-over-quarter and year-over-year growth in earnings, and allowing earnings in one quarter to shoot beyond what is necessary to meet expectations sets a tough baseline for the next quarter and the next year. So CEO's of public companies are increasingly not being rewarded for maximizing earnings, revenue, or growth: they are rewarded for meeting expected targets. If a public corporation misses earnings expectations even by a few pennies in a single quarter, the stock price can fall very rapidly, often losing significant value in a few days. By contrast, the venture-backed startup CEO has no public market to worry about, and no analysts' quarterly earnings forecast to prove correct. What he or she does have are investors who expect to make at least ten times their investment over a period of one to ten years. It is obvious that this drives different decision making behavior as well.

The public company CEO will drive down risk, invest his or her company resources to meet short term earnings expectations, and even go to the trouble of assuring that the company does not earn too much in any quarter. The venture-backed startup CEO will bet on things that maximize the probability that the company will be worth at least ten times more in the fewest number of years. Earnings are not important at the early stages. Much more important is cash flow—the CEO is motivated to get to his targeted capitalization while burning as little cash as possible.

Staffing Function

Finally, the staffing function differs. Traditional information technology companies attempt to reuse their existing staffs of engineers, manufacturing works, sales people, etc., from one product development to the next. If they are unable to do that and have to lay off the staff that was needed for the previous product, they view it as a failure. Human Resources develops career plans for the employees, complete with training programs and even "fast track" programs for the most promising. In venture-backed startups, significant time is allocated to recruiting the right type of talent and experience into key positions. If someone does not measure up to expectations, they are quickly fired and replaced with another recruit. No time is allocated to training, career paths, etc. If the venture fails, everyone is out of work until a new startup is formed with a different team of people selected to meet the specific needs of the new company.

One of the most important effects of these differences is on the decision of which new product developments to undertake. The traditional company is strongly encouraged to select products that are new versions of products they are already producing because they take maximum advantage of the staff and resources that the company already has, and minimize the market and technical risks. Once a new development is started, there is huge pressure on all involved to keep it going: canceled projects do not enhance the careers of anyone involved. Development of a breakthrough product, involving new technology, demanding new talents, aimed at new markets that are changing while the development is underway, and requiring new production resources is not what a manager of a traditional company would stake his or her career prospects on. It is even worse if, as is often the case, the new technology allows an existing product to be produced at a much lower cost, thus threatening the revenue expectations of the current business and disappointing the quarterly financial expectations of the investment community. Better to do everything one can to prevent such a breakthrough product from being introduced into the market.

In contrast, a venture-backed startup is strongly encouraged to only select the development of breakthrough products. The more unstable or ill-defined the market, the better, as long as it shows the prospects of rapid growth. Since the startup management has no existing production resources or staff to attempt to protect, there is no disadvantage of picking a product requiring new talents and production resources. Finally, picking a breakthrough product to develop has the best chance of achieving the venture capitalist's goal of receiving a ten times return on capital. If the company starts to show signs of a high likelihood of failure, then the venture capitalist is prepared to cut his or her losses quickly and go on to the next opportunity.

In times of revolutionary technology-driven change, as happened in the computer and software industries in the 1980's, it is this phenomenon that explains why there was an almost complete shift of leadership. The new leaders were almost all venture-backed startups. When the communications revolution driven by the technology and regulatory shifts currently ripping through that industry is over, the new leaders will also likely be venture-backed startups, that is, unless Lucent, Nortel, Cisco, etc., do something different this time.

Chapter 5

Solutions Analysis: Why the Previous
Attempts to Solve the Problem have Failed

Given these insights into what works and what does not, what are the options that an R&D executive in a large established information technology corporation has when considering a new product development in an effort to avoid the Slingshot Syndrome as described in Chapter 1? The normal course of action is to follow the standard corporate development methodology using standard corporate systems and controls. As we have seen, this works well in stable markets and for follow-on products (i.e. the next version of a current product offered by the company). However, if the markets are not stable, are new or poorly understood, and the product is discontinuous from previous product lines or is a breakthrough product, then the evidence is overwhelming that the standard corporate development methodology and controls will not produce the most competitive product offering in the time frame necessary to be competitive. Loss of market leadership is often the result, and when leadership is lost in enough product lines, the company's longevity itself becomes at stake.

What is the right answer? Various authors have proposed a number of solutions, all of which have been tried in corporate settings, and many of which have worked to a degree of effectiveness; however, none have provided a permanent, successful solution. The following sections analyze each category of these previously proposed solutions and why they are ineffective at breaking The Slingshot Syndrome.

Modifying the Development Methods and Processes

Modifying the development methods and processes is the choice of the process management individuals. Surely the development processes can be modified so that they encourage the development of more new-the-the-world or at least new-to-the-company products. Perhaps a different process for gathering up ideas, funding early prototypes, etc. will make the development methodology competitive with startups. Or, perhaps a special, lightweight version of the corporate methods and processes to be invoked at the discretion of a decision board.

It is safe to predicate that almost every conceivable variation on the standard decision gate development process has been tried in corporate settings. Usually, they produce promising results at first as they generate enthusiasm; however, the initial results invariably go away over time, for a variety of reasons. Either the modifications undermine the controls that are in place to ensure sufficient quality and scheduling issues are addressed, or the initial positive results are really due to the Hawthorn Effect.

The Hawthorn Effect refers to a discovery made by Western Electric in the mid 20th century in their Hawthorn manufacturing plant in Chicago. What they discovered is that virtually *any* change in the manufacturing environment led to higher productivity by the workers over the short term, due to the fact that the experiment itself made the workers feel more important. When they felt important, they were more productive; however, the improvement did not last.

In *Radical Innovation*,[22] the authors showed that successful breakthrough projects tended to have long time horizons and were characterized by starts and stops and periods of going seemingly nowhere. In other words, it is a process engineer's nightmare. Startups address this issue by changing their business plans on a dime and experimenting with customers, unencumbered by corporate decision boards, development methodologies, and cross-functional teams. There is no way that a corporate development methodology can be altered to match this agility without sacrificing what the methodology is meant to do: minimize the risk, improve predictability, constrain functions and features, and coordinate the needed worldwide functions.

Changing the Corporate Culture

Changing the Corporate Culture is the favorite choice of the management consultants. The premise to the solution is that the problem is caused by having an inappropriate corporate culture that does not sufficiently value innovation. All companies have a corporate culture that defines the values of the company and makes it easier for individuals to make decisions that fit within the corporate values and beliefs without the need to consult a leader every time a decision needs to be made. The cultures of mature companies have a strong tendency to value predictability, fiscal controls, quality, etc. above innovation, because that is what their

---

22 Leifer, Richard; McDermott, Christopher M; O'Connor, Gina Colarelli; Peters, Lois S.; Rice, Mark; and Veryzer, Robert W *Radical Innovation: How Mature Companies Can Outsmart Upstarts.* Boston: Harvard Business School Press (2000).

shareholders value (Chapter 2). Even in corporate cultures where innovation is explicitly part of the culture, managers are rewarded more for "making their numbers" (e.g. financial, quality, on-time delivery, schedules) than for introducing breakthrough innovations.

There is abundant evidence that the corporate cultures of large companies do not value innovation very highly. The company management, from the top to the bottom, is almost exclusively focused on operational excellence. Breakthrough innovation is their enemy: it threatens everything that they spend their waking hours trying to control. Breakthrough innovation opens the door to the next generation products that will take the place of their current generation products, which is most always the key contributor to their earnings.

Picture this scenario: an engineer in a large information technology product company has invented a new technology that allows her to implement a product with the same features and function as an existing company product, but for one tenth of the cost, and with ten times the capacity. She makes a proposal to the business unit head of that product line. Let's say that the current annual revenue associated with the product is $15 billion, with a 40% gross margin. His reaction to her proposal will not be positive: in effect she is offering him the opportunity to cut his revenue by 90% to 99%, and cut his costs commensurately, idling most of his factories and R&D staff in the process, and ensuring that he will miss all of his financial targets. When he is done with that "downsizing," the Human Resources department will re-evaluate his position and salary, adjusting them downward to meet his much-reduced level of responsibility. Obviously there is no incentive for him to attempt to commercialize the newly invented technology. Better to attempt to keep the technology from ever seeing the light of day. Patent it to make sure the competition cannot implement the product, thus slowing the commercialization of the innovation down as much as possible.

Clearly, in order to compete effectively head-to-head with startups, the corporate cultures would have to change. But can they, and would the investors allow it? And if so, then how exactly do they go about doing it? Is it possible to implement a corporate culture that makes managers take actions that are not in their own personal best interest? That is what is required in the scenario I just outlined. In my experience, managers will take the necessary actions only when they are convinced that there is no other alternative. What that means is that they will wait until a competitor has introduced products based on the new technology. Then they will wait some more until all of the profit margin has been eaten out of the old product line. Then they will shut it down and attempt to catch up with the competition using the new technology that their own company invented. Often, they never catch up because they did not get an early start on the learning curve, and they end up road-kill in the creative destruction cycle.

One of the interesting questions to contemplate is "what does the investor want to see happen?" Does the investor want the company to launch a cannibalistic attack on its own most profitable products and convert into a new company with a new culture so that it can lead the next wave of products? Or does the investor want the mature company to continue doing what it does best, to ride out the old technology, and die gracefully when it can no longer be milked? Since the investor is perfectly capable of reallocating capital to new startups with the right culture and structure to win with the new technology, why would it be in the investor's interest to have the mature company attempt to reinvent itself, sacrificing revenue and profits in the process? The answer: *It isn't.*

The bottom line is this: it is not in either the stockholder's or the company manager's interest to cannibalize their own product lines with breakthrough innovations. The corporate culture is nothing more than a vehicle to implement these interests—it is not the culprit and thus simply changing it will not solve the problem.

Creating New Business Units

If a new business needs to be created to commercialize a breakthrough innovation, why not do it within the existing corporate structure of a current industry leader? In other words, why not create a new business unit, separate from the other business units producing the maturer product lines. Set up a creative destruction cycle within the corporate boundaries. Would this not serve the investor's interest as well as the corporate management's interest better?

This option has had some success, the most famous example being IBM's PC organization that was set up in Boca Raton, Florida, purposely far from IBM headquarters, and kept a secret from the rest of IBM to avoid any interference. The result was the PC architecture, one of the other great information technology breakthroughs of the 20th century. So it can work. However, once the PC was launched and the Boca Raton operation re-integrated with the corporate controls and systems, nimbler startups started to gain ground on IBM, eventually passing it for market dominance. Dell, a company that started production in a dorm room in 1984, three years after IBM introduced the PC, is now the largest PC maker in the world, leaving IBM in third position behind Compaq. So, at least in this example, although IBM benefited tremendously from the PC division, they might have been able to maintain their initial market leader position to this day if the PC division had stayed completely free of the IBM corporate systems and controls, at least in the fast-growth phases of the market development.

Creating an Internal Incubator

Some companies have set up internal incubators that mimic how stand-alone incubators work. Some have gone as far as to create phantom worlds of venture capitalists, entrepreneurs, startup boards of directors, startup stock option plans, and even carried interest[23] compensation plans for the internal venture capitalists. The concept is to mimic, within the corporation, commercialization approaches that clearly work outside of the corporation.

Although this has produced positive results, it suffers from an inescapable problem: everything that it attempts to emulate about the venture capital and startup environment is not quite as good as the real thing. The entrepreneurs are really still working for the mother ship. The boards of directors are really not boards with legal responsibilities, and are usually staffed with company managers whose corporate experience has not prepared them well for the task. The stock options are not real stock options and the carried interest is not really carried interest. While the purpose is to get the best of both worlds, the result is closer to a poor and inadequate compromise of the two worlds; however, in this type of emulated environment, people do not behave the same way is in the real venture capital and startup environment. They do not think they have the same degree of control or the same degree of risk (and in fact they do not), and as a consequence, they do not make the same kind of decisions. Additionally, if someone is able to pull off a great financial success in this phantom world, the fairness principle of the mother ship's compensation system will intervene and assure that nobody will be able to obtain that level of personal financial gain again. This approach is both noncompetitive and, if successful, self-defeating.

The solution to these problems is to get rid of as much of the "phantom world" as possible and launch the ventures into the real world of real

---

23 "Carried interest" is the term used in the venture capital business to denote the profit split of proceeds from liquidating venture capital investments via IPO's and private sales of the portfolio companies.

startup companies with real boards of directors and real venture capital financing as early as possible. That is the subject of the next chapter.

Starting a Corporate Venture Fund

Corporations have experimented with creating their own venture capital arms. The year 2000 represented the peak of the third wave of corporate venture capital. The previous two waves occurred in the nineteen seventies and eighties. By midyear 2001, almost half of the 245 companies surveyed by Bain & Co. reported that they were terminating their venture funds, indicating that the third wave was experiencing the same fate as the first two waves[24].

At first glance, corporate venture capital makes a lot of sense. If venture-capital backed startups truly have the edge on creating the next breakthrough innovation, why not invest in them using the proven techniques of the venture capital world? The corporation can leverage its understanding of the markets, customers, and technology to bring more to the startup than just capital. It can partner with the startup to give it distribution channels and markets. In return, the corporation gets a front row seat on the viability of the new product and technology. It can become a well-informed acquirer of the startup once it is mature enough to benefit from the corporation's control systems and methodologies. Finally, venture capital investing can become a significant source of revenue and profits for the corporation.

---

24 Whitman, Lou "Intel, AOL, Merck VCs forge ahead." *www.thedeal.com* (October 16, 2001).

Unfortunately, the average duration of a corporate venture capital fund is three years before it is shut down. Three years is not normally thought of as enough time to profitably invest in startups, unless the fund focuses only on the last pre-IPO (a.k.a. mezzanine or bridge) round of funding. So we must look into why, if this is such a good idea, corporations abandon it so quickly.

The average number of years that a CEO of an American public company stays in his or her position is three years as well. What appears to be a good idea to one CEO, CFO, or COO often does not appear to be such a good idea to his or her successor. The reasons vary. Sometimes the corporate venture capitalists are sufficiently successful that they make more money than the CEO's of their companies. At times, the companies become impatient with the funds when all they see are negative returns for the first few years. In other cases, the business units convince the CEO to stop spending valuable capital on outside companies and spend it on their internal business unit projects instead. Occasionally, the analysts refuse to give the corporation any credit for venture capital gains, preferring to value the corporation on its operational results.

The flaw with this logic comes back to the concepts of *patient money* vs. *impatient money.* The investors in a public company have invested impatient money, and they want to see returns on investments in the current quarter or year. Diverting some of that capital into venture capital investments that require patient money does not work—sooner or later the investor will get it diverted back to operational investments. The elimination of the corporate venture fund appears to take about three years on average.

Acquiring Startups

Perhaps corporations should not attempt to create breakthrough products themselves, instead acquiring startups at the point where they would benefit from the controls, procedures, worldwide reach, etc. that the larger corporation can offer. This approach was successfully practiced by H-P, when it acquired Apollo Computers in 1989. That acquisition effectively got H-P into computers in a serious way, creating the basis for what the company is today. Similarly, NCR's purchase of Hawthorne Computers in the 1970's and its acquisition of Teradata in 1993 got the company breakthrough products and technology that turned out to be strategic for what was to follow.

But there have been so many failures that one has to question whether this is money well spent from the investor's standpoint. For example, IBM's purchase of Lotus changed Lotus from a highly regarded thought leader into a second rate product, and rather than giving IBM an office suite with which to challenge Microsoft, it slowed down Lotus sufficiently to allow Microsoft to take a leadership position. Similarly, IBM's purchase of Sequent Computer removed Sequent's NUMA-Q as a serious competitor in servers. One of the quickest failures was Nortel's purchase of Promatory Communications in 2000 for $778 million.[25] Less than 12 months later, Nortel was forced to shut it down, letting go all of the Promatory employees, ceding the rapidly expanding DSL market to Alcatel and others. Another example is Cisco's purchase of Monterey Networks for $500 million in 1999. Cisco purchased Monterey before Monterey's core product development had been completed, and the result was that Cisco ended up scrapping the whole project 20 months later.[26]

One of the differences between NCR and H-P on the one hand and IBM and Nortel on the other is that the former companies had highly decentralized structures at the time of the acquisitions cited. In contrast, IBM and Nortel had highly centralized structures. In the decentralized structures, the new acquisitions could continue functioning with a significant amount of their former autonomy and culture intact, at least at first. In the centralized

25 *The Toronto Star* (June 25, 2001).
26 Quentin, Hardy "Cisco Kidding?" *Forbes Magazine* (May 14, 2001).

structures, this was impossible. The more centralized the acquirer, the faster the key employees left as their employment contracts expired or were rendered impotent within the new corporate structures. What the corporation ends up acquiring, in almost all cases in the information technology industry, is the intellectual property rights to the technology and products developed by the startup, along with sufficient overlap of key employees to train the acquiring corporation's staff on how to produce, maintain, and sell the products involved. The key talent that created the products, company, markets, and technology rarely stays with the acquiring company for longer than a transition period. In the Monterey Networks example, the founders Michael Zidikian and Zareh Baghdasarian left the company within a few months after the acquisition.[27]

One of the problems is that corporations approach the acquisition of startups in the same manner as acquisitions of mature companies. I call the approach "Puzzle M&A," because it reminds me of putting together a jigsaw puzzle. In looking at an acquisition candidate, corporations seek good fits between the two companies. Good fits include geographic coverage, lack of product line and technology overlap, etc. This is an appropriate approach when acquiring mature companies. But when evaluating a startup, they should not be viewing the startup as an equal to the acquiring company. They should view it instead as acquiring the rights and know-how to a new-to-the-world product, technology, or market. Then they need to structure the purchase and the transition in such a way that they assure that they actually get, in good working order, what they purchased.

In many respects, the acquisition of startups in the information technology industry resemble the sale of movies by content providers to distributors in the entertainment industry more than traditional mergers and acquisitions in other industries or with more mature companies. When a

---

27 *Ibid.*

movie is sold by an independent studio to a distributor (e.g. MGM, Time-Warner), the distributor knows that they are acquiring the intellectual property rights, along with contractual commitments by the independent studio and key staff to aid with all aspects of taking the film to market. Note that the distributor will almost always insist on having the right to produce any sequels. Sequels, or follow-on products, as well as associated services, is where most of the revenue is earned in a successful new product, and it is where the strengths of the large, established corporation can be put to good use.

Summary

Although heavily recommended in books, courses, and by management consultants, changing the corporate culture or development process has had no effect on solving the *Slingshot Syndrome* for the simple reason that such a change fails to recognize the reality that public corporations are now run by shareholders who want the corporation to hit quarterly earnings expectations. In other words, the corporate cultures, processes, systems, and controls of most public corporations do a good job of implementing the shareholders wishes with respect to their impatient capital demands. While creating new business units, internal incubators, corporate venture funds, or acquiring startups address the shareholders long term demands for growth, these efforts often fail when implemented inside of a corporation. Therefore, a structure is needed for the industry that is conducive to the expectations of shareholder's long-term and increasingly short-term demands.

Chapter 6

The Solution to the Slingshot Syndrome: What to Do to Get the Best of Both the Corporate and the Startup Worlds

"The [Ford Motor] company began construction of the world's largest industrial complex along the banks of the Rouge River in Dearborn, Michigan, during the late 1910s and early 1920s. The massive Rouge Plant included all the elements needed for automobile production: a steel mill, glass factory, and automobile assembly line. Iron ore and coal were brought in on Great Lakes steamers and by railroad, and were used to produce both iron and steel. Rolling mills, forges, and

assembly shops transformed the steel into springs, axles, and car bodies. Foundries converted iron into engine blocks and cylinder heads that were assembled with other components into engines. By September 1927, all steps in the manufacturing process from refining raw materials to final assembly of the automobile took place at the vast Rouge Plant, characterizing Henry Ford's idea of mass production."

— *From the Henry Ford Museum Web Page*

Information technology corporations, whether computer companies, software companies, or communications equipment companies, all have the same fundamental functional structure, with only a few variations. As pointed out in Chapter 4, the structure harks back to the 19th century structure that founder John Paterson organized the NCR Corporation around in 1884; the same model used by Elisha Grey when forming Western Electric. At that time, there was little infrastructure to support a manufacturing company, so entrepreneurs had to vertically integrate almost every function the company needed within their corporate structures. To such an extreme in fact, both NCR and Western Electric included foundry operations to cast the screws they needed!

However, today's business environment is quite different than it was in the 19th century. In the US, there is an unbelievably diverse infrastructure of business services for sale, and there are active markets for almost every conceivable part and tool. Yet, mature information technology giants have retained a "cookie cutter" structure that has not changed appreciably since Paterson's model. For evidence of this, simply observe the titles of the top management of a company or business unit. Inevitably, you will find a VP of Sales (or Marketing), VP of Engineering (or R&D), VP of Finance (or CFO), VP of Quality, Chief Counsel, VP of Human Resources, and a VP of Manufacturing. Procurement or Supply Line Management may report in at this level or at the next level down. The same applies to the CIO, Public Relations, Research, Support Services, and Professional Services. Additionally, the sales channel is primarily a direct channel, similar to the direct sales approach that Paterson invented. About the only change from Paterson's day is that Manufacturing, Public Relations, Human Resources, Law, and Computer Service may now be outsourced.

New product development (usually a follow-on product) is usually initiated whenever staff is freed up due to the release of a previous product. The features and functions of new products are driven by customer requests, the backlog of unfixed problems of the previous product release, availability of a new generation of parts, features appearing in a competitor's product, and/or cost reductions. On rare occasions the features are driven by a new research breakthrough from the corporate research lab, or, even rarer, a marketing study indicating a new market. Even in the latter case, the marketing study is likely to be focused on estimating demand for a feature that has already been developed for a single customer by Professional Services.

In a typical scenario, the new product development cycle starts with the creation of a cross-functional team with representatives from Project Management, Hardware Engineering, Software Engineering, Systems Engineering, Product Management, Regulatory Compliance, Marketing, Manufacturing, Pre-Sales Support, Global Sales Support, Spare Parts Management, Technical Support Services, Technical Publications, Training, Logistics and Supplier Management. The team puts together a business plan that establishes the features in the product, development schedules, costs, production volumes, markets, and demand. Market size estimates and demand estimates are usually based on a combination of knowledge about current product sales, and secondary market research bought from market researchers. The goal of the business plan is to create a product that can be designed and produced at a profit using existing staff and manufacturing resources. The plan must also be competitive and meet enough of the customer's needs to create the necessary demand.

The business plan is presented to a decision board within the company for a decision on whether to proceed. The decision board prefers plans that make good use of existing resources and can be implemented with as little risk as possible. Representatives of the various functions on the decision board look for plans that fully utilize their functional resources without overtaxing them. Plans where the market is not well understood or where there is significant technology or market risk are not funded unless the decision board feels it has no alternative.

Once the decision board has given a "Go" to the business plan, development begins, parts ordering is scheduled, manufacturing capacity is scheduled, tooling is put into place, services and sales personnel are trained, specific modifications to meet local markets are planned, manuals are written and published, and a promotional campaign is planned. Since the decision board knows that its "Go" will start a significant amount of spending across the company, it is more motivated to reject the business plans that have any risk involved with them. Because of this spending, it is very expensive to stop these processes once they are initiated, and the managers involved end up with chaotic situations to bring back under control. Despite the fact that this is fundamentally a creative process (since new products are being created), creativity is not valued unless it is absolutely needed to get a product out. Therefore, due to their dependence on an existing market, it is no wonder that large, established companies are unlikely to be the leaders when a breakthrough technology changes the game or disrupts that market.

The information technology industry was established and grew up in an era where technological change moved at a snail's pace compared to the current environment. Even in the 1970's, telecommunications gear at Western Electric (now Lucent) was designed with the assumption of a minimum 40 year lifecycle, and mainframe computers were thought to have a 10 to 20 year life. At that time, development cycles for new computers could be up to 12 years long! In contrast, today they are 6 months long. Process control, financial controls, and quality controls were far more important to these giant corporations than creativity, nimbleness and speed.

The Structure of the Creative Industries

Industries where corporations live and die based on their ability to get creative new products in the market, industries such as Film, Recording and Book Publishing, have a different structure than the information technology industry. The creative elements that those industries depend on are not employees of the large corporations—they are independent contractors that feed their wide distribution channels. As in these creative industries, the core strengths of the mature information technology corporations are primarily their distribution channels and associated services.

Let's have a closer look at the Film industry. A typical new product development scenario[28] is as follows: A new movie (i.e. a new product) starts with a screenplay written by an independent contractor, a writer. The screenplay is the movie world's equivalent of a new product business plan. The writer submits his or her screenplay to a number of producers seeking financing. Some producers are completely independent while others are wholly or partially owned by conglomerates that also own a distribution company. One of the producers attaches themselves to the screenplay by acquiring the rights to the screenplay from the writer. The

---

28 There are many variations of this theme in movie production. The larger distributors also produce their own product, films, in addition to acquiring independently financed products. At times, independent producers sell limited rights to a group of distributors or splits worldwide rights between a domestic (North American) distributor and a foreign distributor. But by using an independent writer of the screenplay, an independent producer, and a distribution company, the core capabilities of each participant in the value chain is maximized.

producer lines up the cast, the director, and the financing by enlisting a broad range of individual contractors. Independent producers often line up private equity, similar to venture capital private equity to finance the film's production. Note that the independent producer plays a role similar to that of the venture capitalist, in that he or she reviews the film proposal, lines up financing, recruits the necessary talent, etc.

In the scenario where the producer uses private equity to finance the film's production, the producer sells the distribution rights to a distribution company with the infrastructure to market and promote the film into movie theatres. Such distribution companies include Disney, Sony, Viacom, Fox, Time-Warner, Universal Studios, and Dreamworks.[29] When one of these distribution companies acquires the rights to distribute the film, it also negotiates the rights to develop and distribute sequels and spin-offs of the film. Distribution companies develop and implement the marketing and promotion plan for the film, and distribute the film to movie theatres, home video retailers and TV channels. All of the leading distribution companies are public companies, meaning that they only have direct access to "impatient capital." [30]

A Creative Solution for Information Technology

If we carry this analogy through to the information technology startup, once the initial product has been produced and market tested, the venture capitalist would, instead of liquidating his or her investment via an IPO, look to sell and transfer the intellectual property to a "distribution company" who

29 Standard & Poor's, *Movies and Home Entertainment Industry Survey* (November 11, 2000).

30 See Chapter 2

would have the competence to promote it worldwide, support it worldwide, build it in volume, and develop the "sequels"—follow-on releases and products. Taking this route can be beneficial to the venture capitalist since it lowers risk, obtains a faster liquidation, and reduces dependence on the speculative emotions of the IPO market as well as the tight window of number of IPO's possible. As was pointed out in the previous chapter, when a venture-financed startup is sold to a large mature company such as IBM, NCR, or Unisys it is, in effect, an intellectual property transfer since the entrepreneurial founders rarely stick around in the new company. This is equivalent to the movie industry's value add flow.

In contrast, in the information technology business, nobody in the chain currently thinks that this is the normal flow. Entrepreneurs and venture capitalists normally dream of turning the startup into the next IBM rather than targeting the startup to sell its rights and capabilities to a distribution company, i.e. a large information technology company with worldwide distribution and services capabilities. The "distribution companies" do not see themselves as such, and obsess themselves with attempting to create new-to-the-world products themselves, thereby wasting R&D investment and preventing them from playing the role of eager buyers of the output of startups. When they do buy the rights for new products from startups, they think they are executing "Puzzle M&A" transactions, despite being fully conscience that all of the key entrepreneurial talent of the startups will likely leave once their employment contracts expire.

Richard Caves' 2000 book *Creative Industries* lays out a set of economic properties[31] that together define the creative industries. To investigate whether the information technology industry is comparable to the creative industries, particularly the film industry, and can learn from its history, let

---

31 Richard E. Caves *Creative Industries*, Boston: HBS Press (2000), pp. 1–17

us examine each of Caves' economic properties to determine how well they apply to new-to-the-world product development.

The *Nobody Knows* Property[32]

Caves also calls this the *symmetric ignorance* property. *Nobody knows* whether the customers of a new product of creative industries will like the new product or not. Knowledge about the market, means of production, etc. help, but nobody really knows until it is launched. New-to-the world information technology products have the same property, as witnessed by the fact that the market researchers are unable to correctly estimate market sizes. Note that follow-on products, knockoff products, and sequels do not have this property.

Caves also notes that complex creative products (cinema films, popular music albums) proceed from start to finish in a set of stages, where the costs at each stage are completely sunk before moving to the next stage. This creates an information asymmetry, since information on the product and market may grow as the product moves from stage to stage, and the later stage players have more information than earlier stage players do. Caves believes that this asymmetry explains why in the creative industries the option contract is so heavily used, allowing later stage players the option of not proceeding with the production. Note that venture capitalists funding rounds for new-to-the-world information products also have the opt-out feature for the same reasons.

The *Art for Art's Sake* Property[33]

Caves observes that creative industry workers care about their product to a degree that ordinary workers do not, and will do things that may be of no value to the consumer but will be noticed by fellow artists. In the information technology industry, the analog is *technology for technology's sake.*

---

32 *Ibid.*, pp. 2–3.
33 *Ibid.*, pp.3–4

Anyone who has attempted to manage creative technologists knows that this is a strong principal in the information technology business. The most extreme examples are the people who write destructive computer viruses: they risk their own independence to show off to fellow technologists their cleverness. Less extreme examples are chess playing programs and micro-mouse competitions.

People who believed in *technology for technology's sake* created the Internet, as well as the Unix and Linux operating systems. Many contributors did their work for no compensation or made their work available to all comers for nothing. When the commercial opportunities of the Internet became evident starting in 1994, it was venture-backed startups that jumped on them rather than the integrated information technology companies. Iridium, the Motorola satellite phone system, and G3, the next generation cell phone system supported by European telephone companies, were also *technology for technology's sake* projects, but these were run by very large, integrated corporations. Both can now be classified as enormous financial disasters that could threaten the viability of their corporate backers. In information technology, as in the creative industries, it appears that *technology for technology's sake* projects are best avoided by the large integrated corporations.

The *Motley Crew* Property[34]

The normal assumption that inputs (labor, capital) are substitutable in the production of a product is invalid in the creative industries as indicated by Caves' *Motley Crew* property. Every input must be present at some level of proficiency for a commercially viable product to result. In the development of new information technology products, the same is true, although the effect is more acute in small start-up teams working on new-to-the-world products. Netscape would not have been Netscape nor

---

34 *Ibid.*, pp. 5–6

had the revolutionary effect that it had if Jim Clark had been unable to recruit the Mosaic developers from the University of Illinois Supercomputer Center.

The *Infinite Variety* Principle[35]

Caves notes that there is an infinite variety of products that the creative industries are able to produce and that different consumers entertain different tastes. Therefore, the consumer demands enough variety to fit their varying tastes. In information technology products, there is also an infinite variety of products that can be produced. However, the demand from the customer for variety appears to go through a predictable cycle. When a market is new (say, when the first personal computers appeared), the customers want a variety of products (in this example, both hardware and software). But as the market matures, variety becomes less desirable due to incompatibility problems associated with large variety. Instead, the demand moves to a few products that contain all of the features of the variety of products. Where there were once ten different hardware platforms with different processor chips, the market consolidates onto one. The same is true for spreadsheets, word processors, email programs, databases, etc. This aspect of the *infinite variety* property appears to be unique to the information technology business—where customers once wanted a large variety of different office software, they now want almost exclusively Microsoft Office, but still demand the same set of features that all of the products replaced by Office had. The Internet will go through a similar consolidation.

The *A list / B list* Property[36]

This property refers to the propensity in the creative industries to rank talent onto high priced *A Lists* and lower priced (but still acceptable) *B Lists*. Much effort is expended in the startup phase of a new film to decide

---

35 *Ibid.*, pg. 6
36 *Ibid.*, pg. 7

how much talent to pick from the *A List* versus the *B List*. The information technology industry has the equivalent property in venture-backed startups. Almost all venture capitalists say that they invest primarily in people, meaning *A List* people. But all are realistic and will allow the inclusion of a number of *B List* people in order to control the costs of the project, just like their film industry counterparts do.

The *Time Flies* Principle[37]

In the complex creative industries such as the performing arts and film, this principle holds that once a project is underway, any time delays have the effect of postponing the influx of revenue while costs accumulate quickly. Information technology development projects have exactly the same principle, although the time involved and costs involved can be greater.

The *Ars Longa* Principle[38]

This principle is tied to the fact that many creative products are durable, and the rent (royalties) to be derived from them are durable as well. The legal duration of how long the original creator can collect royalties on the product is the *Ars Longa* principle. In the information technology industry, all participants attempt to protect their creations with patents, trade secrecy, and copyrights. Although licensing of these does produce a royalty stream, licensing revenues are eclipsed in value by direct stock ownership and stock options by the creators in startups who own the patents and copyrights. The durability of the patents, trade secrets and copyrights are key elements in the valuation of a startup, and much effort is expended to protect the durability of all three.

Conclusions

Using Caves' economic principles that define the creative industries, the creation of new-to-the-world information technology products qualifies as a creative industry, with analogous economic characteristics.

---

37 *Ibid.*, pg. 8
38 *Ibid.*, pg. 9

Therefore, it stands to reason that the information technology industry could go through a similar transformation when subjected to similar disruptive forces. As we have seen in this discussion, the stage is now set for exactly this type of change to disintegrate the information technology industry. The effects will be as profound as the 1940's/1950's transformation of the cinema film industry. The advantage that the information technology industry has is that it can see it coming, can see where it leads to, and can take appropriate actions to maximize survival of the enterprise and shareholder value.

Let us suppose that as a result of reading this book, a large and mature information technology corporation decides to restructure itself into a creative organization, feeding new-to-the-world products through its worldwide sales and distribution systems via an ownership stake in startups. How would it look and operate?

The New Corporate Structure Based on Creativity

New Product Development

Rather than attempting to develop new-to-the-world products in-house, under this new model, the corporation will always look to the startup market for new-to-the-world products and markets. It recognizes that venture-backed startups are much more likely to succeed at new product development than the corporation's own in-house development methods, systems and personnel.

The idea for the new product can come from two sources: inside or outside of the corporation. The corporation will require two distinct but related approaches to deal with these two sources of ideas.

Spinning-Out

The first approach applies when the corporation determines that there is an opportunity for a new product. In other words, the source of the idea is from the within the company. The corporation reaches this conclusion as a result of knowledge of its customers and markets and/or as a result of new technological developments in its own research labs or elsewhere. In the ideal situation, the corporation has figured out how to use a new technological breakthrough to create a new market for a new type of product addressing real customer needs. In such a situation, the corporation will create a new startup company, transfer the assets into that company as well as the personnel and intellectual property, and will seek external venture capital investment for the new company. In order to attract the right kind of investment, the corporation will probably have to place the company as a payment-in-kind into a special-purpose venture fund, such as the ones Progeny Ventures runs, taking back a limited partner position in that fund. The general partner of the fund will work with the new venture to recruit an entrepreneurial management team, and once the venture is ready, will organize a first round of venture financing. With the financing secured, the entrepreneurial management team fleshed out and a board of directors is in place, the startup is able to follow the proven methods of business development that make startups so successful at new product and market development.

With this model, through each venture financing round, the parent corporation can maintain its level of ownership by participating in new private equity investment in the special venture fund in which it invested its payment in kind, or it can let the investment be diluted by new investors. It is safe to say, however, that the investing venture capitalists and the parent corporation's CFO will both be happier with a minority ownership level by the parent corporation. Benefits that the investor venture capitalist realizes is a lower threat of lingering controls and interference from a parent majority owner, while the parent's CFO benefits by not having to roll up the expenses of the spinout into the parent's cost structure.

When the new venture has proven that there is a market and has developed its first product, the parent is in an excellent position to buy out the other investors and integrate the venture into its corporate systems and processes using the same approach as described in the next paragraph.

Alternatively, it can liquidate when the venture is sold to another company or is sold in an IPO on a public stock market.

Spinning-In

The second approach, spinning in, applies when the corporation discovers an already formed startup that has proven the market and viability for a new product that the corporation is interested in. In this case the parent acquires the startup from the venture investors.

This is a new, yet not unpracticed art. Private sales (i.e. acquisitions) of startups have become an increasingly popular way for venture capitalists to liquidate their investments. From 1991 through 2000, acquisitions of venture-backed startups grew from 16 to 277 per year, while IPO's of venture-backed startups remained relatively flat around the mean of 192 per year. Even in the "bubble years" of 1999 and 2000, there were only 257 and 232 IPO's respectively of venture-backed startups, both below 1996's peak of 279. In contrast, from 1995 through 2000 venture capitalists raised a record amount of money and invested in over 8,700 startups that were still in their portfolios in 2001.[39] **This information suggests that there are many candidates that will be ready for spin-ins in the next few years and it is in the best interest of the established information technology corporations to actively capitalize on these candidate's need for distribution capabilities.**

The difference between the type of acquisition envisioned here and other M&A transactions is that the corporation knows that it is really buying the rights to produce a new-to-the-world product, and the know-how to effectively sell, service and develop follow-on releases (sequels) of that product. Therefore, to maximize the effectiveness of the spin-in, members of the startup team play training roles in the various corporate

---

39 Charles Fellers, "Making an Exit: VCs Examine their Options", *Venture Capital Journal*, Thompson Financial (May 2001), pg. 40.

functions: Marketing, Sales, Support, and Development. Their role is to train their counterparts sufficiently in an effort to ensure that the counterparts can take over the product and fit it into their corporate processes and systems. Once the training process is completed satisfactorily, the people from the startup earn a bonus and are freed up to go about creating the next new startup, if they so desire. This provides for a clean hand-over without being forced to merge the two incompatible cultures. This method is the equivalent of the film industry's purchase by a distribution company of the rights to a movie from the independent film producer. It provides the maximum leverage of what both the startup and the large corporation are best at, without the confusion caused by viewing the hand-off as a merger. In time, the large corporations and successful entrepreneurs will develop competencies at doing these types of hand-offs well. The ones that become best at it will trounce their competition and easily attract the needed patient and impatient capital as well as the best products from the entrepreneurs and venture capitalists.

Worldwide Sales

The corporation's Worldwide Sales organization becomes the core of the corporation, along with the Worldwide Services organization. The capabilities range from "feet on the street" direct sales forces to indirect sales via resellers, integrators, and retail stores, to online sales and fulfillment via web and call centers, all localized to each country's language and local culture. The winning corporations will have excellent sales support capabilities backing them up, as well as efficient and up-to-date sales force automation or information systems, and information product publishing and promotional capabilities. Inventory management systems and manufacturing scheduling systems linked to data warehouses form the control systems that allow the winning corporation to fine tune product availability and replenishment to up-to-the-day information on orders, sales, and customer interest, thereby tightly coupling supply with demand and strategically focusing promotional activities to stimulate demand. The successful corporation will also have sophisticated financial systems and competencies to deal with currency fluctuations, worldwide tax regulations, and capital flow regulations. Finally, the successful corporation will have expertise at dealing with governments, regulators, and export-import restrictions and regulations.

Although such sophistication, diversity, and worldwide reach may be well established within the large, mature information technology giants, it is very difficult for a startup to develop them on its own, taking many years and heavy investments. Many startups have failed in the transition from a "hot product company" to a worldwide marketing company. By handing off the product rights and know-how to a corporation that already has a sophisticated worldwide sales capability in place, the risk is reduced to both the startup and the large corporation, and the investor's dollars are better spent.

Worldwide Services

The other core capability of the large, mature corporation is its worldwide services organization. Within this category we include on-site "fix it" services, pre-sales and post-sales call center customer support services, spare parts management, refurbishing capabilities, outsourcing services, monitoring services, and professional services. As information technology corporations mature, they have a tendency to increasingly become services organizations. IBM derives 40% of its revenue from services[40], meaning that it is now as much a services company as a computer hardware company. Services have been the main source of revenue growth in IBM since 1990, which indicates that IBM will continue to evolve into a services company and away from being a product producer. Unisys is farther down

---

40 IBM *Q1 2001 Earnings Release*

that evolutionary path already, deriving 69% of its revenue from services.[41] Control Data[42] has evolved the farthest, deriving 100% of its revenue from services.[43] Newer information technology companies such as Cisco, Dell, and Microsoft derive much less of their revenues from services,[44] contracting them out to the more mature corporations.

Like worldwide sales, worldwide services are difficult to set up and get going efficiently for the startup company. Additionally, the management of services is fundamentally different than the management of product development and manufacturing; therefore, a different culture must be developed within the corporation using alternative metrics, methods, systems and objectives to make it run smoothly and profitably. This takes time, money, and patience, none of which a startup has ready access to. The result is that it is logical for the startup to rely on the large, mature information technology companies for the services that are needed to develop the markets for their product, and vise-versa.

Product Line Management

A strong Product Line Management (PLM) organization is necessary for this new style of corporation to succeed. Without it, there is a severe danger that the corporation or its business units would acquire a confusing and nonsensical array of new products via startup acquisitions, thereby confusing the sales force, the customers, and threatening a well-established brand name. The PLM organization's charter is to manage the brand, decide what image that they want the customer to have of the cor-

---

41 Unisys *2000 Annual Report*

42 Now known as Syntegra and owned by British Telecom

43 Syntegra's web page

44 Cisco's, Dell's, and Microsoft's annual reports do not break out services revenue from product revenue, implying that the services revenue is not material

poration, and fill in the necessary individual products via startup acquisitions to support that image. Also, it needs to manage the advertising strategy worldwide and exercise significant influence over the features added in the development of follow-on products. Finally, working with the corporate research lab, PLM plays a critical role defining new product concepts which become candidates for the spinouts described above.

Corporate Research

The Corporate Research lab still may play an important role in this new structure. At minimum, the corporation needs to have the capability of keeping track of the technologies applicable to its markets and products, in an effort to have a well informed view of when new technologies are ready to be introduced into the follow-on products, as well as when new technologies make new-to-the-world products viable. The corporation may find it valuable to go farther than this minimal capability and actually develop and patent some of the most promising technologies, perhaps in conjunction with universities or other research labs. The ability to turn out prototypes of potential products can be very powerful, as we saw in the Xerox PARC case in the first chapter. The additional capability needed in this structure, that is not ordinarily found in corporate research labs, is a capability to incubate promising new concepts and spin them out for venture funding once they are ready for first round financing. The corporation can build this capability in-house, or it can outsource it to a venture capital firm that specializes in such spinouts. By spinning a new product concept out, the corporation gets a very early and beneficial "reality check" from those most experienced with new business development—the venture capitalists. In addition, it allows the corporation to bring in expert help in developing the new business—the entrepreneurs. Finally, it uses a startup business model to bridge the traditional gap between corporate research and development—concepts that are too mature from a research standpoint but too immature from a development standpoint.

Examples

No corporation to date has implemented the full solution being proposed here; however, the following corporations have implemented parts of the solution:

Hewlett-Packard

H-P, under the leadership of CEO Carly Fiorina, has taken some major steps to bolster its core distribution, sales, and services capabilities. Starting in 2000, a corporation-wide restructuring plan was implemented that centralizes sales and marketing for all products into two divisions: consumer products and business products. In 2001 H-P acquired Comdisco's services business the same day that Comdisco declared Chapter 11 bankruptcy (caused by Comdisco's bad corporate venture capital investments), after H-P attempted to buy PricewaterhouseCoopers' professional services business. Also in 2001 H-P announced its intention to acquire Compaq, which among other things would vault H-P into the position of becoming one of the top three IT service providers and expand its worldwide presence to 160 countries.

With its headquarters in the center of Silicon Valley, H-P has significant experience in spin-ins and spinouts of startups. It was the acquisition of Apollo Computers in 1989 that made H-P a serious player in computers. In 2001, H-P acquired Blue Stone Software and StorageApps, two startups whose software products should benefit from H-P's distribution and services capabilities. TimesTen was a technology spinout from H-P in 1996 that turned H-P developed technology into a venture-capital-backed startup where H-P was one of the customers.

Lucent

Lucent established both an internal incubator and an external venture fund in 1998. The internal incubator's charter was to find concepts in Bell Labs that were not being commercialized by the Lucent business units, and to turn them into ventures and spin them out as venture-backed startups.

At the time of this writing, Lucent's internal incubator had spun out 26 such ventures[45] and had spun back in one of them, reclaiming the venture as a part of Lucent. In their external venture fund, Lucent had acquired equity stakes in 48 startups,[46] spinning in (i.e. completely acquiring) one of them. However, in 2001 Lucent found that it was not immune to the stockholder's *impatient money* effects on corporate venture investing, and Lucent's New Venture Group put new investments on hold.[47]

Microsoft

Most of the best known programs in Microsoft's office suite (Microsoft Office) were originally created by startups. Microsoft created Word and Multiplan (which evolved into Excel) when Microsoft itself was still a small startup (1981). Most of the other Microsoft applications suites were built by acquiring single-product startups. FrontPage (acquired in 1996), PowerPoint (1987),[48] SQL Server (acquired as FoxPro in 1992), and Visio (1999) were all independent companies at one point in time. What Microsoft was able to effectively leverage was its international distribution capabilities and brand name to greatly increase the markets for each product, thus turning those Microsoft products into market share leaders and virtual monopolies. In follow-on product releases, Microsoft added features that made objects interchangeable between the applications and allowed them to be compatible with the rest of Microsoft's Office suite and Microsoft's Internet strategy. Microsoft has spent over $1.5 billion since 1994 in over 21 similar acquisitions and has invested over $2.3 billion in minority stakes in over 26 startups.[49]

---

45 Lucent's web site

46 *Ibid.*

47 Aragon, Lawrence "The Smart VC: Bucking the corporate slowdown, part 2." *Red Herring*, (August 8, 2001).

48 The company that developed PowerPoint was actually named Forethought and the one that developed FrontPage was actually named Vermeer.

49 Data from Microsoft's *2000 Annual Report* and various Wall Street Journal articles

Nortel

Under CEO John Roth, Nortel converted itself from a traditional telecommunications equipment company into the leading worldwide distributor for next generation optical technology and data networking-based networks by completing over $22 billion of acquisitions, many of which were startups with revolutionary technology. Nortel has become very practiced at spin-ins, using techniques such as tying payments to meeting market milestones rather than paying for acquisitions when the acquisition actually occurred. That allows Nortel to smooth the transition and gives the founders of the startup incentive to stay and make sure the integration is a success as well as train Nortel regulars on the product, technology, and market. On May 1, 1997, John Roth made it clear that Nortel was shifting from its manufacturing-centric roots: "We no longer describe ourselves as a manufacturer. We consider ourselves an integrator of networks." [50]

Nortel is also experienced in spinouts of new ventures. Entrust spun out in 1997, Elastic Networks in 1998, with Channelware and Saraide following. Nortel now views itself as a "flexible organization able to offer an outlet for entrepreneurial-minded employees, even if their ideas did not fit in with the corporate product program." [51]

Summary

By implementing this new structure, the information technology corporation and startup, whether internal or external, have everything to

---

50 *Toronto Star,* (May 2, 1996), p. E7

51 MacDonald, Larry *Nortel Networks: How Innovation and Vision Created a Network Giant.* Etobicoke, Ontario: Wiley (2001)

gain. The large corporation achieves a steady flow of new products for its distribution channels, services operations, and follow-on product development capabilities. More importantly, the corporation effectively gains access to the "patient capital" needed to develop new products. The result is that the information technology corporation is less vulnerable to being replaced by the next generation of startup turned industry leader.

For the startup entrepreneurs, this structure allows them to do what they do best: move fast, recognize an opportunity in the market and go for it. As opposed to its giant corporate counterparts, the startup can hire when it needs to and fire when it needs to. The startup can address markets that don't exist. It can maneuver its business plan on a dime, enter into a market and then learn what is needed to be successful, and maintain the freedom to pursue any area of potential profitability while fostering a highly creative environment at the time it is most desperately needed. Additionally, a startup can risk it as there is no corporate reputation at stake and it can take on more legal risk than its giant corporate counterparts. The startup has no customer pressure to stay with the current product line; actually, there is not any current product line to defend at all, no manufacturing capacity to fill; no talent base to be allocated. It can grow its markets fast—without being encumbered by the barricades or decision-making bureaucracy of its counterparts. A startup can operate where the large corporation does not dare to go: in areas of high uncertainty, in quickly growing or undefined markets, with risky technology. In other words, a startup can stay small and succeed, handing off the baton to a distribution corporation when the time has come to distribute on a large scale. Then it can start over, again and again. Why should the entrepreneur chance the dangerous path of transforming themselves into giants when they don't need to? Many entrepreneurs and their venture capital backers know that they are much better at the early stage game of creating new companies, products and markets, and not so good at the later stage game of international expansion and the controls and systems that are needed to play worldwide. This approach allows the entrepreneurs to stay in the entrepreneurial game as "serial entrepreneurs," allowing their companies to stay small and succeed, while maximizing and capitalizing on the key strengths of the large corporation. The result is a structure that ensures the success of both the startup and the corporation in the future of technology.

Chapter 7

The Communications Industry: Goliaths at Risk

As we embark on the 21st century, we are witnessing a disruption and transformation taking place in the telecommunications industry. This disruption is unlike any change the industry has faced since its inception in the 19th century. The resulting metamorphosis will be as significant as what the computer industry faced in the 1980's as the result of the PC and the Xerox PARC innovations. As before, the battleground is the North American market. This time, the incumbent leaders in the equipment segment, Nortel, Cisco and Lucent are behaving differently than their computer industry counterparts in the 1980's. The question is whether their different behavior will be sufficient to avoid a replay of the 1980's where new start-ups largely replaced the incumbent leaders in the computer industry.

The telecommunications industry has two major segments: the equipment makers and the carriers. The carriers include local telephone companies, long distance telephone companies, cable operators, cellular telephone operators, DSL service providers, etc. The equipment companies include makers of fiber, cables, circuit switches, PBXs, multiplexors, communications management systems, telephones, modems, packet switches, etc.

The telecommunications equipment oligopoly's actions resemble the actions taken by the major film studios in the 1940's and 1950's, and the situation surrounding those actions has significant parallels. A stable oligopoly of companies is suddenly threatened by regulatory and technological change, and the major players find that they have to completely transform themselves in order to survive. The major film studios, unlike most of the major computer companies in the 1980s, did survive to this day by transforming themselves.

The telecommunications carrier situation resembles the situation that the airlines found themselves in after airline deregulation in the early 1980's. More disturbingly, it also resembles the situation that the railroads found themselves in the latter quarter of the 19th century. Most of the major airlines survived by transforming themselves to meet the new competition. Most of the railroads did not survive the railroad panics of 1873 and 1893.

Five major disruptions are simultaneously effecting the communications industry. The first is the shift from electronic to optical (a.k.a. photonic) technology. The second is the deregulation of the communications services industry (carriers). The third is the shift from operating primarily as a voice business to a data business. The forth is the shift from circuit switching to packet switching. The fifth is the shift from specialized hardware to software running on standard commodity hardware.

These disruptions are all occurring at the same time, creating enormous change in the industry. Communications companies, once viewed as suitable investments for widows and orphans, have become the most speculative of industries. It stands to reason that the corporate structures that were well suited to the previous stable era are no longer suitable for success and survival. On the other hand, the opportunities for creative products and services have never been greater. The explosion of communications equipment startups and internet companies of the late 1990's was only the beginning in what is surely a long-term transformation of the economy into a networked economy. The game has barely started, and the companies who can play leading roles in getting the most creative products and services to market will be the winners.

From Alexander Graham Bell's invention in 1876 until the 1980's, all wire-line (as opposed to wireless or radio) based communications systems used electrical currents to transmit voice and data. The transmission systems were wire, the switches manual (plug boards), then mechanical, electrical, and finally digital. Starting in the 1960's, the wire-based transmission systems were augmented with radio-based ones, both terrestrial point-to-point microwave systems and satellite systems. As we start the 21st century, the transmission systems are becoming primarily fiber optics transmitting light rather than electricity or radio waves. The "last mile" to residential customers is unfortunately still electrical copper wire based—either twisted telephone cable or coaxial cable for cable TV networks. Large businesses, especially in cities, have fiber installed directly to their buildings and it is increasingly being installed within new buildings. The switching and routing systems, however, are still almost entirely electronic, but optical switching and routing technology is starting to enter the market. Optical amplification and multiplexing technology was introduced at the end of the 1990's and is transforming the backbone of the communications network. The first optical switches were introduced in 2000, based on electrically controlled tiny mirrors.

Optical systems have much more capacity than their electronic counterparts, are free of the noise, electrical interference, and cross-talk that plague their electrical and radio counterparts, and are available at much lower costs. In short, optical fiber is a nearly perfect communications medium for stationary point-to-point communications. Although the first optical fiber communications trunks were installed in the early 1980's, technical breakthroughs in the 1990's greatly increased the transmission range and the capacity of fibers. For example, it is now possible to install a transatlantic fiber system that does not require electronic signal regeneration on the ocean floor.

The amount of installed unused bandwidth available in the US fiber optic long distance network was estimated to be around 97% in 2001. One of the reasons for this amazing amount of unused capacity is the fact that fibers take up little space (they have the diameter of a human hair) and are relatively inexpensive, so communications companies find it in their interest to bury many fiber strands at the same time when installing a communications link. Fiber optic cable suppliers were able to cram over 1250 fibers into a single cable in 2001. Each fiber has the bandwidth of 2 terabits per second, or 2 trillion bits per second, yielding a total bandwidth for the cable of over 2500 terabits or trillions of bits per second! The copper cables and microwave radio links being replaced by these fiber cables have bandwidths of 1.5 (T1 carrier) and 45 (T3 carrier) megabits (millions of bits) per second. In other words, the fiber cable available in 2001 had up to 1.7 billion times the bandwidth of the digital transmission lines being replaced! Viewed from a different perspective, if every living human being on planet earth were simultaneously having a telephone conversation with another human being, the bandwidth necessary to support all of those conversations would be 6 billion x 64,000 bits per second = 384 terabits (trillions of bits) per second, meaning that a single fiber cable has the capacity to support 6 planets with a population of the earth all talking at the same time! If voice compression technology were to be employed, the number jumps to 48 planets! Viewed another way, the same cable has enough bandwidth to transmit 62 million HDTV (using MPEG 2 compression) digital television channels simultaneously. New technology is ever increasing the amount of over-capacity by roughly doubling the capacity of fiber cable every 12 months.

This huge increase in performance and capacity started having a disruptive effect on communications industry in the late 1990's. Startup carriers found that the gap between existing prices and the costs of operating a new fiber to be so large that virtually anyone could create a profitable carrier, and many did. All that was needed to establish such a carrier was to run a fiber cable between two cities or even buildings and sell bandwidth to businesses at a price that was below what AT&T, MCI, or one of the Regional Bell Operating Companies was charging. Fibers were strung along rail lines, through sewers, embedded in the middle of high tension power lines, and pulled through natural gas pipelines. The number of Competitive Local Exchange Carriers in the US mushroomed from none in 1995 to over 1300 in 2000.[52] More than $90 billion in new fiber was strung in the United States between 1996 and 2001 alone. The entrenched carriers fought back by stringing their own fiber. All of this activity created a huge demand for fiber, fiber components, optical devices, etc., which Nortel, Alcatel, Lucent, Fujitsu, NEC, Marconi, Cienna, and JDS Uniphase were only too happy to meet. This, together with the "dot.coms" who provided internet services that created demand for the bandwidth, caused the speculative bubble of the late 1990's, which was pricked in April of 2000. The bust that followed wiped out much of the market capitalization of all of the players, big and small, new and old. By 2001, the US telecommunications companies had amassed a debt load of $650 billion, defaulting on over $14 billion of bonds in the first half of 2001 alone. By the fall of 2001, over $60 billion of telecommunications

---

52 Malik, Om "Communications Watch: Five signs of a telecom bottom." *Red Herring*, (August 6, 2001).

bonds were trading at less than 50 cents to the dollar.[53] The three largest Competitive Local Exchange Carriers, Covad Communications, Northpoint Communications and Rhythms NetConnections filed for bankruptcy in 2001,[54] along with Teligent, 360Networks, and Winstar. Metromedia Fiber Networks, XO Communications, and Global Crossing were trading as penny stocks, doing their best to stave off bankruptcy.[55]

Where will this all end? There is no precedence in communications history; however, there are some analogies in other industries that may provide guidance. As I mentioned earlier, in the railroad industry, the initial cost advantage of railroads over competitive carriers (mostly horse drawn carts) was so huge that many people found that building a railroad was a quick road to riches. Over 30,000 miles of track was laid in the US between 1850 and 1873. But they overbuilt in both the US and Europe, causing a spectacular stock market collapse starting in 1873. During the ensuing five years, 89 United States railroads went bankrupt. A second phase of railroad expansion took place between 1878 and 1897. 74,000 miles of track was laid in the United States. A second panic hit in 1893 when 192 United States railroad companies failed. In some countries, the government stepped in and nationalized the railroads, creating the forerunner of their current national railways. In others, consolidation took place until the survivors had natural monopolies over their routes and could stabilize prices.

In the airline industry, deregulation in the early 1980's caused a number of new airlines to be created, all competing with the major carriers on price. One decade later, every new United States airline created since air-

---

53 "Telecom Bust", *National Public Radio Morning Edition*, (August 13, 2001).

54 Young, Shawn, *Wall Street Journal*, August 9, 2001, B1.

55 Futrelle, David "What happened to telecom?" *CNNMoney*, (October 22, 2001).

line deregulation had disappeared. Most went bankrupt, a few were merged into the established carriers. Some of the entrenched carriers of 1984 went away as well—Pan Am and Eastern, while TWA lives on as an American Airlines subsidiary. What happened was that the dominant carriers—United, American, and Delta, figured out how to meet the threat posed by the new cut-rate carriers by consolidating their control over traffic into and out of key airports (Atlanta, Dallas, Chicago for example) while cutting their costs and prices. If a similar pattern were to establish itself in the communication carrier industry, the Regional Bell Operating Companies (RBOCs) who still have strong local monopolies (i.e. a distribution systems) and have preserved or strengthened their services abilities, will survive. So too will the cable companies. The entrenched long-distance carriers will face tough sledding, as TWA and Pan Am did. All of the new entrants since 1996 may become history.

The second major disruption facing the telecommunications industry is the introduction of competition into what was formerly a regulated set of monopolies. The US Telecommunications Act of 1996 had the effect of opening up the local telephone companies to competition, which caused a flurry of new companies to enter the industry, both on the services and the equipment side. Because the new carriers did not have any old base of equipment and no ties to the existing Nortel/Lucent duopoly, they opened up a much more competitive market for equipment startups. The effect was that the old equipment oligopoly (North America—Nortel and Lucent; Japan—NTT; Europe—Alcatel and Ericson) suddenly found that they had serious competition from startups for the first time in a century.

The third major disruption is the shift from voice-dominated communications traffic to data-dominated traffic. The telephone networks had always been engineered to carry voice, with data riding on voice grade circuits. Once it was clear that data would dominate the network of the not-so-distant future, carriers started seriously thinking of building new networks designed for data, with voice riding on top of a data infrastructure.

The fourth major disruption is the shift from circuit switching to packet switching. This shift, caused in part by the realization that data would be the main form of information on the network in the near future, allowed new competitors such as Cisco to enter the market for carrier equipment. Cisco previously had only been able to sell their routers and switches to businesses for their private networks. With carriers new and old adding data routers and switches to carry the fast growing Internet traffic and support the ADSL and Cable Modem broadband extensions into homes and small businesses, Lucent and Nortel suddenly realized that Cisco and startups such as Cienna, Redback and Juniper were serious competitors.

The fifth major disruption is the shift from specialized hardware to software running on standard commodity hardware. The enormous speed improvements of standard computer hardware as a result of Moore's Law has made it possible to consider replacing specialized switching hardware with software running on general purpose computers. Software-based switches, dubbed Softswitches, started to appear in the market at the end of the 20th century. The effect of this shift is analogous to the effect that the PC had on mainframes and minicomputers. The reason is that in the electronics components business, volume rules. If you can design your electronic equipment to use as many high volume components as possible, the costs will be substantially reduced. PC components are the highest volume components in the world, and hence have the best cost-performance characteristics. A PBX or central office switching system based on PC components would have a huge cost advantage over one based on custom components, causing a disruption that favors the startup over the entrenched equipment manufacturer.

Comparison to the Film and Computer Industries

In the 1940's and 1950's the US cinema film industry was threatened by similar disruptions. Their response to the disruptions was to undergo an industry transformation from vertically integrated corporations into one with many specialized players. New product development and how it was financed was radically altered in the process.[56] As we saw in Chapter 6, the film industry has economic characteristics similar to the information technology industry.

Before 1946, the industry was dominated by a stable oligopoly of studios (MGM, RKO, Paramount, Twentieth Century Fox, United Artists, Warner Bros., Columbia, and Universal) who did everything involved in creating, producing, distributing, promoting, and showing new films. They owned all of the assets involved, and employed most of the people or had them under long term contracts (7 years). Production was scheduled a year in advance to assure efficient usage of employees and facilities and a steady stream of new product.

Three major disruptions transformed the film and entertainment industry. The first was the *Paramount* antitrust case against seven major studios decided in 1948. The second was the appearance of a much lower cost distribution channel: television. The third was the invention of portable film cameras. The effect of the *Paramount* decision was that the big studios had to divest themselves of their theater chains. The effect of television was the usurpation of the B-movie distribution to a distribution channel that was inexpensive and widely available directly to the end consumer. The effect of portable film cameras was the enabling of small independent producers who did not own traditional sound stages. With their low cost bread and butter products taken over by television, the film industry had to focus on creating fewer, higher quality, more creative products to attract consumers to the theaters. These disruptions gave independent film producers an advantage over the integrated studios—the number of films produced by independent studios and distributed by the major studios as a percentage of all films distributed by the major studios grew from 20% in 1949 to 57%

---

56 Richard E. Caves *Creative Industries,* Boston: Harvard Business School Press (2000), pgs. 87–102.

in 1957.[57] The studios, in order to survive, had to narrow their focus to the one area where they still had high barriers to entry: the distribution of movies. Although their high margins attracted new competition in the distribution field as well, by 1997 only three of the new entrants remained, and all had been acquired by one of the major studios.[58] Meanwhile, the number of independent production companies increased from 563 in 1966 to 1473 in 1981, with similar proliferation in other specialized film-related firms (Editing, Lighting, Rental Studios, etc.).[59]

The similarities between the film industry of the 1940's and the current information technology industry are striking. In the communications sector, the industry was vertically integrated until the split-up of AT&T in 1996 and the passage of the associated Telecommunications Act of 1996. Before 1996, telephone companies in the US had monopolies over distribution to the end customer for wire-line services, although the customers had been able to pick between competing long distance carriers and cell phone carriers since the mid 1980's. Equipment manufacturers were limited to a stable worldwide oligopoly of Lucent, Ericson, Nortel, Siemens, NTT, and Alcatel, all of which were directly tied in some fashion to one of the large carriers. With the split-up of AT&T in 1996, independent one-product communications equipment companies emerged to compete with the old integrated equipment producers, and independent carriers (CLECs) emerged to compete with the local wire-line carriers. The vertical integration was starting to break down, with serious consequences to the old integrated firms as well as their offspring by 2001.

In the computer hardware sector, the settlement of the IBM antitrust suite in 1982 and the launch of the PC in 1981 by IBM opened up the market to a large number of independent hardware and software companies, at the expense of the then stable oligopoly (IBM, Burroughs, Univac,

---

57 *Ibid.*, pg 94.

58 *Ibid.*, pg 95.

59 *Ibid.*, pg 96

NCR, Control Data, Honeywell). The introduction of the Internet as a commercial channel in the mid 1990's created a free distribution channel for Dell which none of the integrated companies could match in cost. The effect was the withdrawal of the integrated companies from the production and sales of the low cost computers (PCs and servers). The ones who survived (IBM, NCR, and Unisys) refocused on higher value products that could not be efficiently served by the Internet channel, and where their direct sales forces and services capabilities had the most value.

The computer industry went through vertical disintegration at the same time. In 1980, computer manufacturers designed and manufactured their own chips and processors, their own circuit boards, their own mechanical assemblies, as well as their own operating systems, compilers, and application programs. Between 1980 and 2000, they first gave up on making their own chips, then on making their own circuit boards, then on manufacturing the "boxes" altogether. In the software area they gave up on their own operating systems, then their own databases, then their own applications suites. The beneficiaries were horizontal integrators such as Solectron, Intel, Microsoft, and Oracle, all specialists who grew phenomenally as a result.

In the communications equipment business, this type of vertical disintegration has not yet occurred, although it will for the same reasons that it occurred in the computer sector: competition, economies of scale, and customer-driven standardization. As in the computer industry, the customers will force the equipment makers to standardize on common hardware and software components supplied by horizontally integrated specialists. It is in the customer's interest to have this happen, because it lowers their costs due to the enormous economies of scale in chips and software (where almost all of the costs are fixed) and because it gives them freedom of choice by standardizing the interfaces. Vendor-driven standardization efforts do the reverse: they maintain a wide variety of different implementations and incompatibilities to protect the equipment vendor's investments and customer base. With the opening up of the communications equipment market to new competitors and new competitive carriers in 1996, the power in the communications equipment market started to shift towards the customers (both the end customers of the competitive carriers and the carriers themselves), which will force the same type of vertical disintegration as has been experienced by the computer industry starting ten years earlier. Unless the communications equipment producers learn from the computer and film industry precedents, very few of the members of the old oligopoly will still be operating as independent equipment companies by 2010. By 2001, Lucent, Alcatel, Ericson, and Nortel were already showing strains on their financial underpinnings, and all were starting the disintegration process via asset sales.

Chapter 8

Paths of Migration: How Do We Get There?

What actions should an information technology corporation take now to lower the risk of devastation at the hands of a technology, and, better yet, how can corporations take full advantage of these technological and venture capital trends and build on their strengths? The answer depends on the type of corporation.

Category 1: The Mature Information Technology Corporation

This category includes computer, software, and communications equipment corporations that have well-developed worldwide sales and services organizations and highly impatient capital. Examples are IBM, Lucent, NCR, and Unisys.

There are several things that the corporation must achieve to break the Slingshot Syndrome:

- The corporation must close the risk gap between what the R&D Lab produces and what the development organization will accept, more specifically, through accessing patient capital.
- It must, without a home-technology or origin-of-technology bias, feed a superior line of the next generation, new-to-the world products through its world wide distribution systems, thus alleviating a significant competitive disadvantage.
- To be competitive, the corporation must obtain sufficient exclusivity to the next generation's new-to-the-world products that enter their distribution systems.
- It must be able to launch follow-on or sequel products based on its own deep knowledge of its markets and technology.
- It must avoid the trap of expending too much of its resources defending its current generation products, markets, and technology.
- It must solicit and be willing to accept relationships with the next generation of suppliers and achieve the appropriate level of exclusivity with them.

How does it do this? Here is a step-by-step summary of actions that must be taken for a complete transformation:

1.   Corporate Structure: If they are not already centralized, the corporation must separate out its distribution, sales, and services functions from the business units, making them corporate functions or independent business units, as illustrated in Figure 8–1. The product business units become suppliers to the sales business unit or units. This is not as dramatic of a change as it may appear on first glance, because most of the large information technology corporations are already structured this way, or have a structure that is close enough to allow them to get to this structure with relatively minor organization chart surgery. But it is a critical first step, because it creates the enduring core of the going-forward corporation.

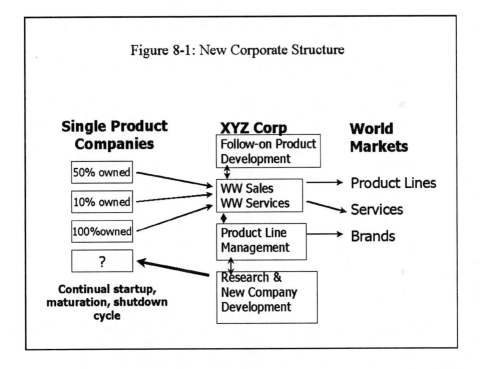

Figure 8-1: New Corporate Structure

2. · Merger and Acquisition (M&A) and licensing practices: These must be revamped to obtain the desired outcomes from startup acquisitions. The revised practices should be focused on acquisition and retention of the intellectual property, training and know-how related to the production, support, sales, and enhancement of the target's products, as opposed to being focused on the retention of the founders and staff.

3. Intellectual property practices: These practices and policies will need revision as well. Incentive systems for encouraging licensing revenue should be reconsidered to make sure they do not create a disincentive to spinning out promising new ventures that cannot generate cash in the immediate timeframe. Broad cross-licensing agreements should also be seriously reconsidered, as they may make the intellectual property of little value to startup investors, who will be looking for barriers to imitation.

4. Research and Prototype development: If it is not already the case, research and prototype development should be centralized and made a corporate function. As we shall discuss later in this chapter, the corporate research lab plays a key role in the creation of new-to-the-world products. By maintaining this capability in the core, the company has the ability to take advantage of new technology breakthroughs to create new partially owned startups that meet real customer needs in its markets.

5. Product Line Management (PLM): If there is not already one, a centralized organization should be created and put in control of what products the sales organization markets. This creates the control point for what products to offer, what new products to add via startup acquisition, what new startups to spin out as a result of new technology or markets, and what the company brand represents.

6. Business Units: The current product business units should be at least partially divested. Exclusive arrangements should be included, where needed, for the markets that the PLM organization is targeting. The business units benefit from being allowed to go after other markets, and the parent corporation becomes free from the feeling that it has to keep the business units and their product lines alive at all costs.

7. Spinout Incubator: If the corporation does not already have one, an incubator should be created to spin out new startups based on ideas and technologies from within the corporation. This incubator needs to be focused on spinning out startups at the earliest stage, rather than attempting to emulate a venture and entrepreneurial environment inside the corporation. This function can be partially or completely out-sourced to a venture spinout specialist, but it requires a powerful internal champion to make it work.

Category 2: The Consulting, Outsourcing Services and Systems Integration Companies with Worldwide Reach

This category includes system integrators such as Accenture and SAIC, outsourcers such as EDS, and in the communications industry service providers such as AT&T and Williams Communications who already have a global services reach. By adding a startup acquisition and spinout capabilities, these companies may be able to get to the distribution company model first, ahead of the traditional computer and communications equipment companies. A number already have experience incubating startups and participating in venture capital investing.

The functions and systems that are missing in these corporations are the needed product development systems, as well as the controls and disciplines to do an effective job of follow-on release development. Also, their sales forces and systems may not be optimized for worldwide product sales and distribution. Finally, their current business revenue and profits may be heavily tied to relationships that could be threatened if they were to move into the product business themselves with competing products. One option to seriously consider is merging with a company who does have the missing capabilities (i.e. companies who have strong development capabilities and distribution capabilities, but not professional services capabilities, e.g. Cisco, Microsoft, Dell, H-P).

Category 3: The Startups Turned Global Companies

This category includes ten to twenty year-old hardware and software corporations that have grown into very large and valuable companies with global reach. Examples include Microsoft, Dell, Cisco, and Compaq. These companies face the same three issues as their more mature counterparts, listed above. The difference is that they may lack sufficient maturity in their worldwide sales and services capabilities, something they may have partially or completely contracted out. This may force them to play a different role than their more mature counterparts.

Dell, for example, has a powerful direct sales system via the Internet. Rather than simply focusing on PC's and servers, Dell is in an excellent position to turn this competence into a distribution powerhouse for a broader range of information technology products by following the steps outlined above for mature corporations. Microsoft is in a similar position for packaged software sales and distribution, using their excellent software integration, packaging, localization, training and promotion capabilities, as well as their close ties to retailers worldwide. On the threat side, Dell, Microsoft and Cisco are in danger of over investing in their current, mature products (PC's, Office suite software, routers) rather than investing in the next generation of products to use their excellent sales, distribution, and follow-on development capabilities for. In other words, they are subject to the same threat that their more mature counterparts have experienced and which has at times led to their corporate extinction.

Category 4: The Young Startups

This category includes startups that are at some stage of developing a breakthrough information technology product, i.e. a product characterized by high uncertainty in multiple dimensions. Products that are new-to-the world, are focused on new, rapidly changing, or poorly understood markets, and/or have high technology risk fit into this category. For reasons that we have discussed in Chapter 4, startups face no serious competition from the established players with this type of product. However, once the market and technology risks have been reduced, the startup is at a severe disadvantage to its established counterpart in doing all of the necessary things to produce, distribute, and support their product or products in volume throughout many countries while maintaining high quality. A friendly acquisition by a company who can act as a distribution channel for the product maximizes the risk/reward formula for all involved and places the product into the most competitive position in the least amount of time.

Unfortunately, the number of problem-free integrations of acquired startups with their acquirer is very small. Too often, the acquiring company brings the startup to a standstill by restructuring it, replacing redundant functions, and imposing the acquirer's corporate culture, controls, and systems on the previously successful startup. The mistake is to treat the acquisition of a startup the same way as an acquisition of a mature business. In the latter case, the point of the exercise is to merge together two separate business structures into one, with a combination of both businesses fitting seamlessly together into a new whole. Therefore, it makes sense to quickly reorganize so that the complementary business processes can work together, while they obtain the economies of replacing the redundant functions. In the startup case, the point of the exercise is for the acquiring company to learn how to produce, sell, maintain, and extend a new product. Because the startup is past its creative stage and is now in its expansion stage, the culture of the startup is no longer applicable and need not be maintained after the merger. An arrangement with the personnel of the startup to transfer their knowledge as quickly as possible needs to be part of the acquisition terms. The founders may also need to be involved in some of the promotional activities when the product is launched in various markets. Once the distribution company is trained, the startup personnel may choose to reestablish themselves as a new startup to produce the next breakthrough product.

Strategic Spinouts

Spinning out startups as a *strategic action* is a relatively new concept for information technology corporations. Spinouts of non-strategic technologies and business developments have been around for a while. H-P, NCR, IBM, SAIC and Lucent have all done non-strategic spinouts. Sometimes the parents doing the spinouts regard them as consolation prizes to a research team where the parent has decided not to proceed with further funding. Sometimes they view it as a way of liquidating *stranded assets*, i.e. intellectual property that is the result of R&D that the parent has decided not to commercialize. Spinouts of startups are an excellent way to do this, and often the only way of getting a financial return from the R&D investment of those non-strategic products.

A few leading-edge companies are starting to consider strategic spinouts, i.e. spinning out startups as a new way of driving shareholder value, and perhaps the only way of commercializing their R&D investments in new-to-the-world technologies and products. These companies include Battelle, Sarnoff, SAIC, SRI, CSIRO (Australia), and Progeny Ventures.

By doing strategic spinouts, the parent corporations gain access to *patient capital* to develop a new business concept or new-to-the-world product. If the spinout is successful, they can buy out the other investors and spin it back in—exactly like a startup acquisition. Another option is to maintain strategic relationships with it as an independent company.

The Future Roll of the Research Lab

While large, mature information technology companies have not demonstrated the ability to develop new-to-the-world products for the reasons cited in Chapter 4, their research labs have played a very important role in developing all of the technological breakthroughs of the last half-century. Figures 3–7 and 3–8 shows how research work bounced back and forth between government-funded research primarily at universities and corporate research labs, before being commercialized. Note that commercialization was often not led by the company funding the research.

A recent study by Richard Foster and Sarah Kaplan of McKinsey & Co. of more than 1000 companies over a 36 year period showed that in the telecommunications sector, there was no correlation between R&D spending and total return to the shareholders. Additionally, in the computer hardware, software, and semiconductor sectors, there was actually a negative correlation![60] In other words, the more spent on R&D, the lower the return to investors. With the investors money in corporations growing increasingly impatient, the corporation that figures out how to commercialize the technology coming out of its own research lab by using patient money and startup approaches has the potential of trouncing its competition; hence the growing interest in strategic spinouts.

---

60 Richard Foster and Sarah Kaplan *Creative Destruction,* New York: Currency Doubleday (2001), pg. 213.

The historical, anecdotal, statistical, and experiential evidence adds up to the conclusion that while corporate research plays a key role in developing breakthrough technologies, the corporations funding the research have found it very difficult to capture the advantage from their investment. The problem is that the most successful model for commercializing new technology is not found within the corporation and cannot survive within the corporation due to the inherent contradictions with corporate controls, incentives and systems cited in Chapter 4. Attempting to hand off research directly from the corporate research lab to a business unit's development organization (that has been optimized around follow-on release development) rarely produces market-leading breakthrough products. One of the key reasons is that the business units' decision process often uses "hurdle rates" that require new products to have positive return on investments within 18 to 24 months (or to become cash-flow neutral in a similar period). Contrast this with venture-backed startups, where for the 1999 IPO's the median time between the first venture funding and IPO or acquisition was eight years for non-Internet related startups, five years for Internet-related ones, and only one third of the startups were profitable at the time of the IPO or sale.[61] In other words, the venture capitalists and their limited partner investors are willing to wait more than eight years for profits.

Given the increasingly short term demands for returns on investment, it is unlikely that boards of directors of Category 1 corporations would hire a CEO who would commission risky development projects with an explicit up-front expectation for profitability of more that eight years. Yet the evidence above shows that for breakthrough products to emerge, it takes just that, a risky development project with duel ignorance, on the part of the consumer and the inventor, that a market for the product even

---

61 Data extracted from the VentureOne and VentureExpert databases

exists. Modifying the hurdle rates in the standard decision processes will therefore not solve the problem: the corporations funding the research need access to the patient capital and associated processes and systems where the investors *are* willing to wait over eight years for profits.

Accessing Patient Money

The first thing that such a company needs is access to the patient money. As we have seen in Chapter 2, the only form of patient money available for technology commercialization now is venture capital. Fortunately, there is a lot of it. In fact, at the current rate of growth, the total amount of venture capital available in the United States will exceed the total investment in US corporate research in the 2000's; however, it is difficult, if not unrealizable for a public corporation to obtain direct access to venture capital patient money. Only through highly specialized methods and corporate revisions can it be done. As we saw in Chapter 4, the venture-backed startup management approach is radically different than the corporate approach, and for very good reasons that have been learned the hard way over more than a half century. This fundamental incompatibility between the nature of the startup and the nature of the corporation prevents the corporation from attracting patient money investment from the investors. Additionally, it prevents the venture capitalists from investing directly in projects that are under the governance, controls, and systems of the corporation. Therefore, corporations cannot obtain any direct patient money funding from either their investors or the venture capitalists.

A way to enable this approach is to create a company that is organized along the lines of a traditional venture capital fund, but is completely focused on creating new startups out of internal corporate projects. After the projects are spun off, the new ventures are funded, staffed, controlled, and compensated identically to other venture-backed startups. What is unique is that the "parent" company benefits financially and in some circumstances strategically if the venture is successful. Consequently, the parent companies can use this approach to develop new businesses that they either want to partially own or buy back from the other ("patient money") investors after they become sufficiently mature.

Figure 8–2 shows how this can be structured. What one does is create a new company for the internal venture. The people, assets, and intellectual property are transferred into the new, separate company, and venture financing is then sought to grow and develop that company. The parent company becomes a passive limited partner in one of the funds that owns the new company. The outcome of this structural maneuver is the best of both the corporate and the startup worlds.

Since the governance of the spun-out venture is separated out from the parent company, relieving the parent of the responsibilities associated with managing the venture funding rounds and everything that goes with that, it makes little difference whether the parent is "high tech" or "low tech." The deciding questions for a successful spinout are: (1) does the new venture meet the criteria necessary to attract venture capital investment, and (2) is the business in an area in which venture capitalists are currently investing? On question (1), Progeny Ventures, for example, uses a screen of 19 questions to validate that the proposed venture qualifies as a candidate for venture funding. On question (2), Progeny takes a look at where venture capitalists are currently investing, including polling the ones that are the most likely interested investors. Where venture capitalists invest changes over time, and is in the process of changing at this moment. So a real-time poll is necessary to see if there is interest at the time when a spinout is being considered.

In order to attract venture capital and the right kind of entrepreneurial talent, it is important that the parent company play only a silent limited partner role. With the structure illustrated in Figure 8–2, the parent can attract the necessary venture capital and choose to keep whatever level of ownership it likes by selecting its level of participation in each financing round. Upon liquidation, it can choose to participate in the financial gain of an IPO or private sale, or can choose to buy the venture back itself.

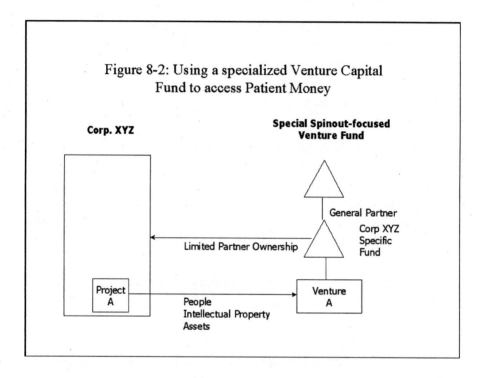

Figure 8-2: Using a specialized Venture Capital Fund to access Patient Money

Progeny Ventures' approach is to create a new fund for each parent corporation to hold their "progeny." This allows each parent to add new spinouts to their fund at any time, as well as dedicate additional funds at any time, so that they can control the amount of dilution in each funding round. Multiple venture capitalists compete in the funding rounds, so the parent company gets the best deal that is available at the time of the funding round. Typically, right after the spinout or coincident with it, Progeny Ventures arranges a funding round and looks for a third party venture capital firm to lead it. If there are multiple candidates, Progeny goes for the best deal to the parent. Normally the lead venture capitalist will syndicate the round, meaning that it is open for other venture capitalists to invest in for a limited period of time.

ActivityPath, a spinout facilitated by Progeny Ventures, illustrates how it works. ActivityPath was a project within a major information technology corporation that, while promising, was not viewed as being in that company's strategic intent. It created a new-to-the-world product using advanced imaging technology for which no defined market existed yet. Essentially, ActivityPath's technology is able to track how people move around inside buildings, how long they stand in lines, etc. The target market includes retailers, banks, airlines, and consumer goods manufacturers who want to better understand how consumers behave in a retail environment. It is a perfect example of something that should do better in the startup world than in the corporate world. Progeny Ventures created the ActivityPath company, put the intellectual property, assets, and project members into it, created Progeny Venture Fund I with the parent company as the sole limited partner, transferred ActivityPath into the fund, and started a search for venture capital. In this case, we discovered that by merging ActivityPath with two other startups, we could create a more fundable company with a more complete management team and set of talents, and therefore a better chance at success. Only a few months after creating the company, we merged it, taking back shares in the merged entity now known as Emtera. Note that this type of merger would have been much more difficult to do, if not impossible, if ActivityPath had stayed within the parent company.

Corporations decide not to further invest in projects for many reasons, sometimes unrelated to the viability of the project or potential business. Some of these rejected projects become excellent prospects for turning into stand-alone businesses. Corporations should consider spinning off some of their strategic initiatives as well, to give them the nimbleness to compete effectively against other startups where nimbleness is needed.

Summary

Transitioning to the solution described in Chapter 6 requires some structural changes that differ depending on the type and maturity of the company. It can be accomplished in a series of steps making for an orderly transition. Corporations who go through this transition will be the survivors and winners, able to attract both the impatient and patient capital that they require, and fielding the best product lineups worldwide. They will become magnets for venture capitalists to sell their best startups to, and will also become magnets for the best talent.

Chapter 9

Tales of the Transition

Due to the fact that I am proposing and predicting a structure for the information technology industry that does not exist as of the writing of the book, it may be difficult for you, the reader, to envision how this new world works, and what it will be like to be part of it. The purpose of this chapter is to help you understand this new world via fictional stories about individuals leading their corporations through the envisioned transition. All characters and companies in these stories are fictional—any resemblance to real people and companies is purely coincidental.

Betting on Risk: A new CEO, 2002

Hugh Garrison tapped the pencil eraser on his white front tooth and glanced down into his cold coffee mug, looking for answers.

"They just won't take it. The company is too far gone by now. She's our best shot at success." Hugh continued to tap as Martin Gregory, a venture capitalist he had worked closely with over the past ten years, continued to read the candidate's profile.

"Hugh, she is Mark Porter's daughter, you know, the guy who reengineered MGM in the second half of the 1940's. She has managed to follow in his footsteps rather well. After all, she saved six technology startups from bankruptcy by working out distribution deals with corporations in exchange for minority equity stakes. Her profile neglects to mention that, but I worked personally with her on two of those deals. I know she's good."

Both Martin and Hugh were outside directors of M. Collins Corporation, a major information technology company that has had the reputation of a friendly corporate giant for over nine decades, setting the precedence for many technology companies to follow. Both men were the key advisors for the committee's CEO recommendation and all eyes were on them: the media, the stockholders, the board, and virtually every single employee of the company.

The conference room table was covered with profiles of candidates and rejection letters, scattered across the brutal WSJ headlines: "M. Collins Corporation sells assets to pay down debt burden;" "M. Collins Corporation one notch above junk credit rating;" "M. Collins Corporation Cutting work force by 35%." In all of Hugh's years on the committee for CalPERS, he has never personally seen a company in such poor shape. His strong fiduciary duty to his policyholders was forcing him to seek creative options in an effort to make the company succeed and thus pull CalPERS' investment out of the gutter. That is the only reason he would have ever considered a candidate like Mary Anne Porter for the job.

As far as the new CEO nomination was concerned, Hugh realized that his vote was unofficially the official decision. The board vote was simply a formality after this special committee's recommendation. Martin reassured him, "We really don't have a shot at getting Breckenmyer, he's with IBM now and happily situated."

"Well," Hugh sat up straight and combed his silver and black hair away from his eyes, then rubbed his blue eyes with his index fingers, "let's bring her in and make the recommendation. I believe she's right for it Martin. You know her best. She really is our only shot, isn't she?"

The board members were gathered around the cherry conference table, all nine men were dressed in suits and ties, chatting and munching over white powdered donuts. The scent of morning coffee and sharp aftershave lingered about the conference room, which was catching the Monday morning sun through the double paned glass. The busy room grew quiet as the young redhead walked across the wide isle to her chair, coffee in hand and bagel in tow. She removed her blue blazer jacket and hung it gently on the back of her chair. Hugh approached her first and extended his hand, "Mary Anne, I am so excited you are going to take it. You will have our full backing during this meeting and throughout your tenure, no matter what your plans are. We are betting on you, your experience and your credentials."

Mary Anne smiled and extended her hand. "Thank you Hugh. I do appreciate your support. But I haven't said yes yet."

Hugh smiled and returned to his seat as the chief legal council called the meeting to order.

Immediately following the formalities of the introductions, the chairman of the board Frank Wilright, spoke to the members smiling back at him. "I am very pleased to introduce the committee's fine selection of Chief Executive Officer, Mary Anne Porter." The room exploded with applause. Mary Anne didn't blush. She knew how fickle this kind of crowd could be.

"For those of you who don't know her, and there aren't many in this room I am sure, Mary Anne Porter was formerly one of the leading venture capitalists in Silicon Valley and she has certainly made a name for herself over the past fifteen years in the business." Frank waved a Fortune Magazine cover around, Mary Anne's bright smile beamed from the cover. "Two years ago, she was one of the top three most powerful business women in America, and just last month, Business Week profiled her previous venture fund portfolio as one of the only survivors in this depressed stock market we all know so much about."

Another round of applause, and this time, Mary Anne blushed slightly at the sight of the Fortune Magazine cover. "We are very pleased to have her here at the company in such a time of difficulty, to say the least. Now, allow me to introduce her, Ms. Mary Anne Porter."

Mary Anne stood up to speak for yet another explosive applause, embarrassed but not fazed. "Thank you all, thank you very much. Frank, thank you for your kind words. I know this meeting is mostly a formality, but I do not want to take this job unless I get some things straight." The room grew frighteningly still and Mary Anne realized it was about to lose the formality.

"I know how to fix this company, but I don't know how many of you in this room are going to like it."

Frank quickly interjected, "Ms. Porter, you see, we are prepared to give you six months to analyze the problems and return to us with a proposal on how to fix them."

Mary Anne smiled kindly as she addressed his offer, "That is very generous of you all. But I don't need six months to figure out what's wrong, and frankly, you don't have that luxury. Before I would agree to take any job, whether as CEO of a technology company or real estate office manager, I want to know exactly how I can help the company succeed better than before. I know what the problems are and I have solutions that give this company the greatest chance at success, despite what the press is saying at the moment."

Mary Anne looked to the group for questions. Hugh Garrison urged her to continue, "Please tell us what you have in mind. I think we are all pretty open minded to any solution at this point."

"Certainly. Basically, everyone who reads any local newspaper knows that this company has been penned for dead, abandoned and forsaken. Yet, several years ago, it was the darling of Wall Street. Since that time, the young startups have eaten the market share of the old products and yes, this company is extremely slow and traditional in its commercialization approaches. While pronouncing M. Collins Corporation dead may sell more newspapers, I don't believe it to be true. When I look at the core of the company, the true value of what this company has to offer, it isn't the technology at all. It is the worldwide sales and distribution systems that have been established in over 130 countries for more than eighty years. Working with startups for the past ten years, I have seen how establishing distribution and sales channels can kill very promising technologies within months. Startups who don't have their distribution channel operational at the time of their growth phase greatly reduce their chance of survival. And with the technological forefront ever changing, this company will need to maneuver fast, react to changes, implement solutions and deliver promising results in time for quarterly stockholder's increasingly impatient expectations. I have news for everyone here: making this company competitive with startups in developing new-to-the-world products is impossible. There is a basic paradox that this company can never surpass. So my solution is to quit trying to maneuver like a startup because this company is not a startup. However, it has qualities that a startup desperately needs. My solution is to take advantage of the company's maturity, its methodical ways of doing business, its dependable business practices, and still meet those quarterly expectations. It will take a new structure and over five years for it to work properly, but just like a good diet and exercise program, you will see healthy results, slowly at first, and then increasing satisfactory results will follow."

"Well, that's one hell of a pitch, but I don't know how you are going to do it. Tell us exactly what your plan is Mary Anne." Hugh Garrison sipped his coffee at the end of his sentence, not sure if he should have put her on the spot so quickly. "Or if you like, you can prepare a presentation on PresentationPoint and present it to us next week." He was definitely testing her out, not her plan. It was important she was the right kind of person for this job, and better to find out now than later.

Mary Anne stood up and accepted his challenge. "No, I don't need to prepare a presentation. Excuse me, is there a white board in the room?" Hugh tapped the window next to him and moments later an administrative assistant entered the room with dry erase markers and an eraser. The assistant pulled the string on the bottom of the screen and jumped back at the snap of the screen rolling upward, revealing a white board behind it.

"Thank you very much," Mary Anne added as the assistant cleaned the existing blue marks from the last meeting.

"Look, based on the premise that this company will never be as fast as a startup, it will never survive in the current market as such. That's just common sense. So, either the company needs to figure out a way to become fast, or it needs to switch markets. M. Collins Corporation knows its markets and sales channel better than some of us know our own children, so switching markets is out of the question. So how does M. Collins Corporation become fast? How does it act like a startup without becoming one? To know the answer to that, one must also analyze why the industry is changing so rapidly and what it all means to M. Collins Corporation. There are a plethora of reasons why the industry is changing, but the accelerating change in technology is commanding an increasing premium on creativity. Manufacturing is no longer a necessary core competence. Increased outsourcing allows new approaches to be possible, as does increased specialization. Now what do we do about it?"

The board sat quietly and listened to her speak. Her confidence was contagious and some of the other members began to feel like the company wasn't going to crash into the ground after all.

"Well, there are a couple of issues right off the top that need to be taken care of. First of all, the PC business this company is in is causing more problems than anything. The junk bond status credit rating can be attributed to the deterioration of the PC division, and I am willing to bet on that. The cost of producing the PCs is now higher than the sales price. The company is far behind in business to consumer direct sales through e-commerce, forcing all sales to go through retailers, causing M. Collins Corporation's products to not only become dated on the shelves, but carry prices dictated by the retailer. And the retailers are getting a high margin as well, don't forget, which detracts from our profits. The ailing PC division must be exited immediately. The price war is only going to make things worse. This company, or any company for that matter, cannot afford to be dragged down with such a hemorrhaging division."

Not a single board member could argue with the recommendation. The last CEO was fired because of the ailing PC division, and he refused to get rid of the excess capacity.

Hugh spoke for the room, "Mary Anne, that is a perfectly logical first step. I believe I can speak for the entire board when I say that is a good decision and we all back you up completely."

Mark Sayberg interjected, "So you're saying once we exit PC's we should be fine?"

Mary Anne continued without directly addressing Mark's comment, only turning her green eyes in his direction. "Even if the company would have exited PC's years ago, it still would be in trouble today for a few reasons. One of the reasons is due to the inevitable reality that startups will always be faster and more maneuverable than a large corporation when it comes to commercializing new-to-the-world products. While this has been a normal trend throughout history, if it can be avoided, an investor will not tolerate it happening to his or her investment. Based on last year's annual report, M. Collins Corporation spent $400 million dollars on Research and Development. About 20% of that is for Research, 80% for Development. Not one feature or product from Research made it into the current product line. The commercialization probability of the technology in Research is virtually at 0%. Development has little if any communication with Research and vice versa. The result is that the company becomes blindsided when the newcomer who recognizes an opportunity to develop and commercialize the next generation product seizes its markets. This company is not making any new-to-the-world products for its customer base, and because of it, M. Collins Corporation is slowly, but clearly, losing customers. Yet, $400 million dollars a year is spent keeping up with current technology to prevent this from happening.

Mark Sayberg interrupted her rudely again, this time with a surprisingly accusatory tone, "So how do we keep our customers? How does the company put the newest products through their distribution system successfully? Mary Anne you can't cut R&D. I think I know where you are going with your recommendation. You may or may not realize it, but this company's identity is engrained in the R&D of new technologies. You take that away, you take away more than just a lab."

"Mark, I really don't think you know exactly where I am going with this, and I am not suggesting R&D be cut, not the funding amount anyway, rather the way we fund it. There is a negative correlation between the amount spent on R&D and the amount on the bottom line. And not to mention the fact that the more I look at it, it appears M. Collins Corporation's investors are paying $400 million dollars in overhead for gadget shows and awards that generate no revenues in return. The company's current decision gate process won't let any new-to-the-world products through anyway, for the most part because they don't have a defined market yet."

"Well, why would M. Collins Corporation have a system like that—it doesn't make any sense." Hugh asked directly, speaking for many of the newly educated board members.

"You see gentlemen, the market doesn't exist because it is still being developed, which is why it is called a new-to-the-world product. The commercialization techniques for developing-market products are much different from what is necessary for the development of follow-on products. It's just something this company is not prepared to handle. I believe M. Collins Corporation should spin out the most promising investments, maintain a percentage ownership in each of them, and spin in startups in their growth phase, through a similar reverse process, placing the next new-to-the-world technologies through M. Collins Corporation worldwide distribution systems. The technologies being spun out need a completely different atmosphere to survive and prosper. Not the one M. Collins Corporation is currently providing them. In less than ten years, the research lab could be self-supporting. As a first step, I propose we take $100 million dollars of the R&D dollars and spin out our technologies into startup technology companies."

"Interesting concept. We may need to think about it though." Hugh Garrison was intrigued by the notion, and he was sure she was right. "Where would the whole process begin? I mean, do we just jump in there and start spinning stuff out? How do you envision that happening?"

Before she could answer, Mark Sayberg interjected rudely. "Researchers are not entrepreneurs. It would never work."

"Good point Mark, and Hugh, I think I can address both comments at once. There are specialists that can work with the researchers in the lab to identify what technologies can successfully spin out into the private equity markets. These specialists are part venture capitalist and part researchers themselves. They understand the technologies, but also the business side of things. Then, they take a percentage of the profits if there are any, through an equity stake in the spinouts. They will recruit the necessary management and provide assistance in gaining funding for the new companies."

George Sand, the CFO, interjected this time, "How is this treated? The equity? As a capital account? How exactly does this affect the books? Will that $100 million be taken as an immediate charge?"

"It will show up on the balance sheet as a private equity investment. I suggest the investment be accounted for at cost, what was invested in the technology, until a funding round occurs. Then it can be marked to the market value." George seemed content with Mary Anne's answer.

The soon-to-be CEO continued her explanation, "Basically, instead of developing technologies that aren't going to be used, the research lab will learn to develop companies to spin off into the private equity markets."

Mark interrupted again with more agitation than before: "But why would we spin off our best technologies? It just doesn't make any sense to me. We wouldn't be a technology company any more."

"True. But if you don't, you run the very high risk of not being a company at all any more due to the lack of new-to-the-world products running through the distribution system. Not to mention the fact that you are cutting the funding on them anyway because they aren't contributing to current revenue fast enough. Might as well get some value out of them."

Martin Gregory spoke this time, in Mary Anne's defense. He, a fellow venture capitalist, understood exactly what she was trying to do and it all made perfect sense to him with his nontraditional business ideals. "She has a point, Mark. This plan focuses the company around the core value add, the distribution system, sales force, and services associated with the products, not around the ever-changing technology. It allows the technology to come to the company, the best and without an internal company bias on what goes through the sales channel. It opens the company's markets for purchasing the best technologies and putting them through their distribution systems because the BU's[62] are not forced to put internally generated technologies through the system. Additionally, it gives the brilliant ideas inside of Research a chance for commercialization and puts their funds to a much better use."

Mary Anne spoke up, adding to Martin Gregory's support: "The result is better products going through the sales channel, while those same prod-

---

62 Business Units

ucts are able to enter into other markets where we don't operate nor have any desire to sell, which increases our margins and revenues. The bottom line is: this company needs to generate revenue growth and positive earnings growth."

Several other board members grew increasingly interested and wondered about the details of her plan. Howard Malone, the former CEO of a food distribution company questioned: "How would the deal to spin in work? Would we license the ability to sell the products?"

"Yes and no. Most likely, the company would spin in startups that are in their growth stage, needing a strong distribution force. In some cases, we would structure a deal whereby we end up with full rights to the intellectual property of the product, and the people are obligated with incentives to train our developers, support personnel, professional services people, and sales people on the product. Once the training period is over, the founders would be free to join M. Collins Corporation or go off and create another startup.

"In other cases it may make sense to only own a percentage of the company, acting as a reseller for the startup with an exclusive market seller agreement, while participating in the financial success as an investor. By having a stake in the companies, M. Collins Corporation can keep them from running around the sales channel once a market is created. Look at what happened with Cisco. M. Collins Corporation created the market and then Cisco sold around it. M. Collins Corporation would have been much better off had they taken an investor stake in Cisco. If M. Collins Corporation had bought Cisco and integrated it into the company, it wouldn't be the Cisco it is today, the fast moving highflying stock performer we now know it as. M. Collins Corporation would have killed it instantly with a controlling 'corporate culture.'"

Mary Anne must have hit a few nerves on the board because she noticed several members grimace at the memory.

"I am sure there will be more done, once I ascertain other problems. These are just the large surface issues that are running the company into the ground rapidly."

Uncertain faces stared back at her. She wasn't sure if her blunt report had put the members in shock. Hugh and Martin were the only ones showing any signs of comprehension. It was certainly an earful, but a hopeful one. Mary Anne decided she would challenge their uncertainty.

"Look, there really isn't much option here. I am not going to do this thing unless I have your total support. I have to implement this thing completely, not partially, or it won't work. I will certainly ask for your expert advice, but I do not want to waste my time making presentations and getting approvals for this structure. Either bet on me or don't bet at all. I will say this, I have saved dozens of companies from bankruptcy and complete devastation over the years, and if you want to see this thing live, you are going to have to do something radical, something risky and new. Either you let me implement this plan and give this company a chance of survival or I walk out the door. I didn't select you. You selected me. It won't work, or even have a chance of working, unless I have full control of this company and full support from each of you."

The chairman kindly disagreed with her governance stipulations and attempted to gain momentum by speaking much to fast. "Well you see Mary Anne, we prefer to have a vote on large company decisions." Before she missed a beat, Mary Anne shot back at him, "Yes Frank, and see where it has gotten you. I will appeal to your best judgement and advice, but bet on me, Frank, not the plan. You now know the details and can either take them or leave them. It's up to you."

Hugh Garrison stood up from the glass topped conference table. All eyes in the boardroom focused on him. "And all this from reading some annual reports." The deep fluctuations in his voice gave away his approval of her plan to the rest of the board members, even if his eyes didn't. "Pretty impressive Ms. Porter. I'm going to have to say I admire her boldness and courage. I am willing to bet any company on that. If anything else, this company is going to need that to survive."

The vote was unanimous and Mary Anne shook the hands of the board as they exited the room, tongue-tied and stunned into radical submission.

The Spinout, 2002

"I knew it couldn't be this easy. Not even close." Mark O'Bryan thought as he slammed down the black telephone receiver. "What was I thinking? How does anyone deal with this corporate bureaucracy?"

He let the weight of his head rest heavily in the palm of his hand while massaging his forehead deep in thought. The telephone's shrill ring woke him from his temporary state of sanity.

"This is Mark O'Bryan. Oh, Hello Mary Anne—uh, we need to talk."

"Sure Mark, what's up? I was just calling to see how the spinout is going. Did you tell the guys today about the plan?"

"Yes, and I think they took it OK. Tomorrow I am introducing them to Kevin Melbourne, the new CEO I hand picked for the spinout, who is flying in from Sydney, and Angelica Diosiono, the new CFO. I think they should all get along nicely. And then we are going to look at the new office space in Research Park."

"Sounds great. So tell me, why do you sound so disturbed?"

"Mary Anne, I realize that you are new to the company, but when you brought me in to do this deal, I never thought it would be so difficult. I just hung up the phone with Jay Gallagher, your VP of Finance. He told the legal department to stop working on the separate company structure paperwork and he vetoed the compensation package we agreed to weeks ago. The internal corporate council working on the deal won't return my calls now. Jay said that he couldn't approve any deal that gave researchers the ability to make more than the CEO. He told me my scheme was ridiculous and unheard of and he hung up the phone on me. He is quite an emotional guy I'm afraid. You are going to have to call him to get this thing straight. The controller is going nuts with my budgeting requests—they aren't making any sense to him because he doesn't understand a venture fund structure and he doesn't believe me when I calmly explained it to him, several times. Oh, and while you're at it, please call Gina Morgan, your VP of intellectual property because I think she has stopped the asset transfer into the shell company until she personally hears from you."

With a reassuring smile from the other end of the receiver, Mary Anne replied, "Well, I knew this thing was bound to tie up sooner or later. We of all people know what it is like to get things done outside of the established protocol. Most people just don't know what to do, Mark. On top of that, the whole company is in a state of shock right now. Most of them are somewhere between anger and denial that the current way of doing business must change for the company to survive. And not only that, most of the upper management and some of the middle managers are afraid they won't have a job tomorrow, so it's understandable. I'll call Jay and Gina and try to figure out what is happening and I'll take care of it. Don't worry about the implementation of what I said, I haven't forgotten how the deal is supposed to work. It may take more time than we are used to for everyone else to adjust to all of the new changes, but once we establish precedence, they will grow to support it. Chaos is not quite at hand, Mark, although it may feel like it trying to get this kind of deal done."

"Thank you, Mary Anne. I have learned something from doing this before with you. You are amazingly calm and rational about this."

"Mark, you and I both know that calmly and rationally is the only way this kind of thing will get done. Call me if you have any more problems."

"Thanks again, Mary Anne." Mark couldn't believe that spinning out this one little technology that the former CEO had already cut would be so difficult.

Without Mary Anne on my side, this could never get done, ever.

As soon as Mark hung up the phone, it rang again. Only this time it was Michael Gordon, one of the founding technologists of the spinout.

"Hello Mark. We may have a problem. Jonathan is ready to leave the mother ship for the spinout, giving up his stock options and everything, but his wife is having second thoughts about it. And you didn't hear it from me, but she just found out she is pregnant with their first child. I think you ought to talk to both of them to get this stuff straight."

Mark realized this was a much larger problem than the ones he was dealing with earlier in the day. If the key technologists wouldn't go with the spinout, no investor would ever fund it and the whole deal would fall through.

He reclined back in his black leather chair and stared out of his office window, which overlooked downtown Chicago. He thought out the day's events while Michael spoke. It was one obstacle after the next. First the internal company patent attorney offered considerable resistance to the intellectual property transfer, then the Vice President of Finance refused to sign off on the carried interest incentive compensation for the venture capitalists, and now this, the employees weren't sure if they were ready to leave with the spinout.

The project would never get external funding without the founders, the ones who designed the technology. The developers are an essential piece of the management team and the success of the project hangs on their ability to work closely with the new CEO and CFO. No one else knows the technology better than Michael Gordon and Jonathan Mitchell. Michael and Jonathan are both top-notch technologists, two of the best the company has, and it would be a loss to their department if and when they both left with the spinout; however, Mark saw something different about them, something extraordinarily ambitious and entrepreneurial. They belong with the startup and they both share a sense of ownership of the technology. If they did not go with the spinout and stayed with the lab, they would eventually see a pattern that Mark had observed many years earlier before he was a venture capitalist, when he ran a research lab for AT&T. The frustrating and sometimes cutting reality of corporate research life is at times rather difficult to take for a researcher who pours their heart and soul into a project. He observed time and time again the cuts in funding because not enough new-to-the-world projects were contributing current revenue fast enough. There was little if any coordination between Research and the Development of new products, which had over the years stifled any hopes of rapid commercialization. Mark witnessed projects that he personally started and were continued by fellow researchers simply shrivel up and die inside the walls of the lab while a less extraordinary version gained worldwide acceptance as an industry standard. These circumstances have made technologists like Jonathan and Michael leave before, but at least this time it was going to be done correctly.

He continued his thoughts while Michael talked. Mark decided if this thing was going to be fixed, it needed to be done so as soon as possible.

"Michael, perhaps we should have a meeting about it. Would tonight work? I want to take the two of you out for dinner. My treat. Please tell Jonathan to bring his wife."

"Can we do Italian?"

"Sure, we can do Italian. Is Rossi's at 8:00 alright?"

"Sure, I'll check with Jonathan but if you don't hear back from me then plan on meeting us there."

"Great. I'll see you then. Thanks again Michael." Mark hung up the phone and looked out the window in his office, wondering how he was going to handle this one. It is more difficult than usual because Mark is too familiar with the scenario. This was such a sensitive issue—divorces are a scary reality for any career change and Mark wanted Jonathan to succeed in business without having to sacrifice his family.

Mark arrived at Rossi's at 7:48PM, but was the last to be seated. As he arrived with the maitre d' at the table, he noticed the tension between the three young adults, who couldn't be a day over twenty-five. Jonathan was seated beside his wife and was fiddling with his buttons on a neatly pressed white shirt, while Michael was nervously munching on a bread roll. Amanda was staring off into a distant thought, twirling her blonde tendrils around a perfectly manicured rose-colored index fingernail. As

Mark approached the table, Michael and Jonathan rose awkwardly to greet him, "Hello. We uh, both got here a bit early." Jonathan added as they all took their seats. Mark's gentle voice and comfortable smile eased the tension at the table immediately

"Hello Amanda. How are you tonight? You look lovely."

"Thanks Mark. I'm OK, well, considering the circumstances."

"Well, that's what I wanted to talk to you about tonight. That is why I invited the three of you here. We need to talk about the details of the spinout."

Amanda interjected before he could get another word in edgewise. "I just don't understand. Why can't he stay with the company? Why does he have to leave? Can't the project just hire him temporarily as a contractor or something?" She turned to her husband as her voice rose to the tone of a plea. "Honey, didn't you used to do something like that for the company?"

Jonathan looked embarrassed at her primitive understanding of his occupation, but he calmly corrected her misunderstanding. "Yes, I used to be a contractor, but I can't do that with this company. Michael and I personally designed all of the technology and the company wants to quit paying for it anymore. But it is really good technology, stuff that a lot of people can use every day. The technology is called facial recognition technology and it will eventually eliminate the need for any kind of identification cards or credit cards. So the next time you lose your purse, it won't be that big of a deal. We only have to replace your makeup and your favorite chewing gum."

Amanda smiled as a small chuckle escaped her pursed crimson lips as Jonathan continued. "Only it won't be ready as fast as the company wants it to be, and even if it was, the market, those people who would buy it, don't know they need it yet."

"Oh, I see." Amanda was starting to understand the whole picture a little bit better, but Mark could tell that she still wasn't content with her husband being thrown from the deceptively protective corporate arms of the company into the cruel harsh reality of startup businesses.

Amanda turned to Mark with interrogating eyes. "Mark, tell me one thing, what will it be like? How will we live if the company doesn't make it through another round of financing?"

Mark wasn't shocked by her blunt approach. He was rather relieved she was getting down to the meat of the details. Before he was able to answer she asked another question, indicating that she had given the matter some thought. "But can't he have a contract saying that if this thing doesn't work out, he can come back to work for the company?"

Mark had anticipated this kind of question as well. Amanda needed to understand the reasons behind it or she would have no reason to think the deal fair.

"No, not exactly. You see Michael and Jonathan and some other people we are hiring are starting a new company, separate from the corporation they now work for. We need them to be completely dedicated to the success of that new company. We could offer them a job back here if it does-n't work out, but if they needed that kind of safety net then they really aren't the kind of people we need for the job anyway. It is going to be risky, and it may fail, but if they leave, they must take the full responsibility and ownership of that risk."

"Excuse me, may I take your order now?" The waiter, dressed in all black with a silver serving tray in hand, had been standing at the edge of the white linen for at least five minutes, but no one had seemed to notice.

After they ordered their vegetable lasagna, crab, and steak, Mark continued with the thought, not missing a beat. "Amanda, please tell me why you don't want Jonathan to leave the company to become an entrepreneur with the technology he developed?"

"Because, I am pregnant with our first child and our family needs the stability, not the risk."

As Mark cut his salad he addressed her anxiety. "Amanda, that is a very valid fear. But also know his compensation rewards that fear. Your husband will own a significant portion of the business he has helped to create. The upside is limitless."

"You mean he would be the CEO?" Mark knew it to be a difficult matter to convince the founding technologists that they may not be the right kind of leader to run the new company, but explaining to their wives was a different story entirely.

"Right now, tomorrow actually, Jonathan and Michael are going to meet Kevin Melbourne and Angelica Diosiono. They are going to help them run the new start up, but Kevin will be the CEO and Angelica will be the CFO. Both have run startups in this stage successfully for many years and I have the utmost confidence in the two of them. I think your husband and Michael play a better role as CTO and Chief Architect, where their strengths can be realized fully."

"I suppose so," Amanda looked doubtfully at her plate, "But, won't he be missing out on incredible opportunities with M. Collins?" Mark smiled at Jonathan.

"Maybe you should answer that one." Jonathan turned his blue eyes towards Amanda's and held her hand in his. "I feel I would be missing out more if I didn't go. I really believe in what I am doing. And I know I will regret it if I don't go."

The server placed the dinner on the table, but the attention was centered on Jonathan and his wife.

"I just don't know Jonathan, I just don't know." Amanda added softly as she quickly excused herself from the table for the ladies room. Jonathan followed closely behind her. Mark glanced at Michael and spoke wisely:

"Michael, I don't know if it is worth it. I will talk to the venture capitalists and see we can work something out."

But before he could finish, Michael cut him off. "Mark, first of all, you know the VC's won't go for it. Second of all, this kind of thing is going to happen every time you try to do a spin out at M. Collins Corporation. Do you realize that? So if you set this 'something to fall back on' precedent, it will haunt you every time the situation occurs. Either he is committed to go or he is not. No safety net, no fall back plan. All or nothing. Survival or not. It's just that simple. Look at what happened at Enitude Corporation with their 'phantom' program. No one was truly committed to the new companies they created; only the stability of the mother ship. He has to be willing to take the risk, and besides, if he stays at M. Collins, he will be miserable every time he pours his heart into a project just to see it get cut, and then witness another one just like it—only not as good—become commercialized by a different company and made into an industry standard." Michael drank a long gulp of water after he spoke his peace. Jonathan was not only his coworker, but also a friend, and him not going with the spinout would certainly put tension on their friendship.

Amanda returned to the table, with red-rimmed eyes and holding Jonathan's hand. The four dinners were cold with time, waiting anxiously on Jonathan and Amanda's return. They sat down and faced Mark. Amanda spoke first, "I want him to go with the spinout. He's right. You're all right. It will be much better for everyone involved if the two of you work together on it."

For the first time all day, Mark was flabbergasted and didn't know what to say, not from anger and frustration but from pleasant surprise. She appeared to have turned around 180 degrees in his favor. He wondered what Jonathan must have said to her to make her change her mind.

As they left the restaurant that night, Jonathan stopped Mark on the way out.

"Thank you for helping me with this. I believe in the technology's success so much I am willing to do almost anything to stay with it. I am just glad I don't have to sacrifice my family in the process. Amanda and I have been through tough times in college before, financially speaking, so we know can do it again, even if it is with one extra person on the way."

Mark smiled at the thought of a baby in this whole mess.

"It won't be easy Jonathan, but it will certainly be an interesting experience."

The first of his Kind: A Visionary CIO
July 16, 2008[63]
Written by Lane Morton, technology business
reporter for CIO Magazine

How the CIO of Airoecraft Corporation, George Bunching, turned his company into an information technology powerhouse, and how he has made millions in the process.

In less than one year, his net worth increased 5000%. At this rate, CIO George Bunching will be a billionaire in two years. Two years! And to just think he almost turned down the not-so-dreamy job of CIO for Airoecraft, a second tier Airline equipment manufacturing company at the time, for a senior Vice President position at IBM. In hindsight, he made the right decision, but at the time, IBM was offering a base salary $100,000 above what Airoecraft was offering him. Why would someone with a technology focused background stay with a second rate airplane manufacturing company for considerably less money? That's what we set out to discover in our interview last month with the soon to be richest CIO ever.

He insisted we meet in a coffee shop at LAX on the busiest weekend of the year for flying: Labor Day. Parking was a nightmare as the traffic outside the airport was horrendous to say the least. We met on the Delta terminal of the airport, Gate 6. Delta, a former front runner in air travel, was packed with travelers running and frantically trying to make their gate. Employees were scrambling to make a paper check-in system work, asking for picture identification while questioning "have your bags been with you at all times?" Apparently, the situation was made considerably worse by a

---

63 Fictional Headline

glitch in Delta's computer system's new software (ironically enough, the new software was designed to speed up the whole process). The glitch caused the entire system to crash. Lines formed at every nook and cranny and red jackets were seen running along side them, desperately trying to accommodate the influx of people into their non-functioning terminal ticketing gates. While trying to cross into the coffee shop, I almost lost an arm as I fell victim to a middle-aged woman running frantically to her gate, car seat in tow.

George was seated calmly in the back corner against a large window; Delta planes nestled busily behind him. He was reading a Market Street Journal and sipping on a bottle of water. He must have been sitting there for some time, despite the fact that I was thirty minutes early. He had already leafed through the first two sections and was about to close the paper when I sat down next to him. George is in great physical shape for a man of nearly fifty-six and contributes it to his "morning walks to the lake and back with his wife and two trips to the gym per week." This guy must get up at 4:00 AM.

"Mr. Bunching, this place is a mad house." I looked to him for agreement as I took the seat next to him.

"Yes. It is. And please, here and in that article of yours, call me George. Would you like to go to a quieter location for the interview?" George was reading my mind.

"Sure, if you know of a better place." And, much to my mistaking, I added pessimistically, "It's Labor Day weekend and I think just about every corner of LAX will be slammed jammed with people and traffic."

George just grinned back as he rolled his paper with his left hand. "Well, I think I know of a place. Grab your things, and let's walk over to the Meridian terminal."

Ten minutes later, we were entering Terminal 2, Meridian Airlines. Unlike the Delta terminal, the cars outside weren't beeping and honking their way through to the appropriate drop off location. Black sedan's lined the side streets and stretch limousines were parked systematically. George walked calmly past them, and I followed. Inside was something completely different as well. The scene was something I had only dreamed of: it was a peaceful haven. No lines. No red coats running around yelling frustrated and angry, yet there were just as many people, if not more, in the terminal gates. The passengers were of the business class, mostly in suits, some in business casual attire. They were loading onto their flights quickly and without delays. Even the coffee shop was quieter, and safer to walk into, I might add.

"Wow. This is incredible. You would never even know it was the busiest flying day of the year unless you looked outside or in another terminal gate."

George just grinned again and sat down in a similar spot; this time, he selected a booth with his back to the wall, facing the passing travelers. "Wait until you see the planes."

He smiled back at me and offered to buy me water or coffee. I gladly accepted under my awe of his demonstration.

"It really is incredible, George." I told him, "the condition of the terminal. It's like someone developed the perfect order for flying." That someone was George Bunching.

Six years ago, George didn't want the job as CIO. "I always believed it was an acronym for 'Career Is Over.' I was scared to death when it was offered to me." A rising star within his company, George was ready to leave Airoecraft at the time for a career at IBM where he was offered a high paying, senior level Vice President of Software position. But something changed his mind, something last minute and unexpected. "While researching the CIO job for Airoecraft, I ran across an article written by a venture capitalist who was spinning things out of a major information technology company. He was advocating that large companies should consider spinning off their best technologies, and he cited one particular spinout that I found quite interesting." At first, George admits he was pessimistic about the idea. "Why would Airoecraft ever benefit from spinning out their top projects?" He added. Unexpectedly, the funding for one of the projects he was working on was cut because it wasn't contributing to current revenue fast enough.

"But that was because it was a new-to-the-world product that was being created for a market that didn't exist yet, but I knew soon would. I thought, if only this project could get outside funding to stay alive, Airoecraft would see that they made a mistake and would understand how useful the technology would be for them. And the project would live, saving the effort and funds already dumped into its creation. It was because of that project that I understood what the venture capitalist was talking about. It was because of my understanding of the concepts that would save Airoecraft's future that I stayed."

George developed a vision of how to help the company and how Airoecraft could become the world's leader in airline information technology without any additional effort or funds. One afternoon, George and the CEO had a 'chat' about this vision for the company and the role it would play in the future of technology.

"I told him that if he wanted me to take the job as CIO, he had to let me do things my way, which meant I was going to implement a risky and newly developed plan. He had to allow me to implement this plan that risked the core of the company: our customers. But, if the plan worked, and it has, I promised him that it would propel Airoecraft to the primary seat in airline information technology development and deployment. It would be an unprecedented victory. I saw a unique opportunity to do something great. I almost didn't stay. If the CEO hadn't agreed to do things differently, allowing me to implement my plan for the future of the company in technology, then I was going to leave. It was that simple."

CEO Mike McGlaughlin bought his proposition and virtually gave George free reign to implement his plan, which has redefined air travel and technology as we know it today, less than a decade later. The plan allowed the company to lead this technological revolution, and in the process, they created a highly profitable subsidiary to pave the way.

The first thing George did was open up the company, dissecting every project and piece of information technology in the research and development pipe.

"Since I had been working there for almost three years, I already knew a substantial amount of information about Airoecraft, and what could improve the company's chances of long term success."

At that time, Airoecraft had some of the greatest inventions George had ever seen. Inventions that far exceeded anything that was actually being put into the planes. They were inventions that would change the paradigm for flying forever.

"These inventions were being wasted in our labs and in 'shows for clever inventions.' I stepped back and looked at the picture as a whole and decided if there was any room for me to maneuver and make something work for the company. We had and still have the largest database in the world. We had the customer base and the supplier base that was needed; Airoecraft was in the best position to create an information technology revolution.

"After researching the processes of venture capital and how spinouts were performed, I worked with venture capitalists and 'angel' investors to isolate several ventures that would meet the external funding criteria of private equity investments. I worked with the team of developers to create a business plan for the spinout ventures that were competitive for venture capital funding.

"Additionally, new companies, shell companies really, were established to accommodate the spinouts. The people, assets and intellectual property were transferred into the new company; Airoecraft continued to work with venture capitalists to get the startup company placed into a venture capital fund as a payment-in-kind, in return for a limited partner ownership stake by Airoecraft." To align interests, a side-by-side fund was created for top management's personal investment, the fund where George has earned millions of personal dollars.

The venture capitalists that Airoecraft worked with recruited top-notch entrepreneurial management teams for the spinouts and conducted funding rounds to obtain the necessary operating capital.

The result was the development and commercialization of the premiere passenger identification, information and scheduling system linked to a powerful data warehouse and interconnected to new state-of-the-art systems and equipment within the aircraft. With a strict market focus, George saw another unique opportunity unfolding. The creation of an airline that created demand for these new products, focusing on the class of travelers who needed them most: the business and elite class. George spotted the problems from the time he first entered corporate America, with long flight delays, unreliable travel, inferior if any access to business communication equipment (like email and internet access) to use while waiting. After considerable review, Airoecraft agreed that the business venture would not only stimulate demand, but would not greatly interfere with the immediate business of their customers, the airlines, who were the lifeblood of Airoecraft's bottom line at the time, and still contribute a significant amount to this day.

Thus Meridian Airlines was born; all first class and fully equipped with the newest technological advancements in airline travel, including the ability to upgrade that technology with minimal capital. Meridian Airlines, the Airoecraft subsidiary, focuses mainly on services to the upper business elite, flying only into major cities and offering connecting services upon request. Not a price leader, Meridian's flights are not cheap; however, they are guaranteed against technical difficulty. With backup planes waiting in the wings, flights are never canceled. No waiting, flights are regularly scheduled and are always on time, with the exception of weather delays. The flights are also priced rationally; every posted flight is the same price for every purchaser, and you can calculate your flight from Chicago to Tokyo by adding the Chicago to New York flight and the New York to Tokyo flight price. Alternatively, you could take the three times a week direct flight to Tokyo. Taxes are included and transportation to and from the airport is included, up to 30 miles. Anything further than that can be arranged prior to the flight and is an additional cost per car, not per passenger. The prices reflect these advantages, almost 30% higher than other price-war flights on Delta or United Airlines. So why would anyone pay such inflated prices? The answer is simple. Travelers are fed up with the services currently offered by airlines. The long lines, unreliability, poor security and the prices that don't make any sense: that's why it is worth it. Companies are willing to pay for the extra time their employees can work while traveling, in addition to the increased security and reliability of their flights arriving on time. Full Internet access on every corner of the terminal for no extra fee. Full access to telephones, fax machines, email, and WebPages personalized to each passenger while flying. One cannot even enter the Meridian Airlines terminal without a Meridian "boarding pass," also known as a facial recognition clearance.

"The lines have been reduced by nearly 88% because of our facial recognition technology. That was the key complaint by business passengers on four of the five major airlines five years ago and remains the same today. Oh, and it just so happens that this was the technology that I read about in the article by the venture capitalist; combined with what we were working on at the time, we developed the technology to what it is now. And the technology we combined it with was the cut project I was working on before I took the CIO role at Airoecraft. It's amazing: out of two severed projects from different industries, airline travel was revolutionized forever."

Ten years ago, and still to some degree today, the airlines were entering into price wars with one another. Airoecraft was manufacturing top-of-the-line, new products to be put into the planes; however the funding for these projects were being discontinued because there was no real market for them in terms of airline purchases. The airlines weren't purchasing the new and needed equipment because they were ignoring customer demands and needs. They were so concerned about keeping costs at a minimum that they were neglecting their highest margin, moneymaking consumer: the business and first class travelers. They were too preoccupied fighting for the bottom-rung travelers, the price sensitive, that they lost sight of the top. And this affected their chief supplier, Airoecraft.

Airoecraft was being forced to produce what the airlines were buying and not what was in demand by the consumers. Airoecraft conducted a study using consumer-monitoring technology and discovered that the airlines had it all wrong. The airlines operated as if all passengers simply wanted to sit on the plane and eat pretzels while watching the same movies. They thought that the access to communication devices was sufficient for business travelers. It wasn't. Business travelers' chief complaint was their waste of time: the lines at the parking drop off; the lines at the baggage check in; the lines at the metal detectors; the lines entering the plane. At each bottleneck, large gaps of time were wasted. A thirty-minute flight time was expanded to a four-hour ordeal, if the plane took off at all or on time. Basically, the airports are designed for the maximum convenience of the airlines and rental cars, and for the maximum inconvenience of the passengers. Additionally, the camaraderie that the business and first class once shared is now left to a dull void, as the seats in business and first class are almost always reserved for frequent flyer upgrades and are rarely actually occupied by business travelers. The business class complained of the interruptions they received on the aircraft during flight time by those who weren't working, rather guzzling the free drinks and bothering them with useless conversation, only second to wasting time at the bottlenecks. Not to mention the fact that all travelers are virtually out of any communication while flying. One frenzied airline traveler called flying his 'dead' zone. Meridian is changing that.

As a result of the cuts in R&D funding for the advanced research on products that would define the future of the aircraft due to the airline price wars, and the obvious business class discontent, Airoecraft CIO George Bunching took notice of a unique opportunity within the company.

"Airoecraft can't do much about the actual in-air time, but we can make the experience better and more useful to the business class and first class travelers. The most time is wasted in the process of getting to the airport, boarding, and then sitting on the aircraft out of communication with the world. Not every passenger is the same, they are very unique and have unique needs. It is time an airline recognized that."

George underwent a massive study using pattern recognition technology to find out where people spent their time in the airports and how they behaved. Using a mathematical optimization model, George worked with Airoecraft's top technologists and methodically sought out to remove the bottlenecks, thus developing a plan that introduces the necessary technology to fix them. Based on these findings, Airoecraft has revolutionized the flying paradigm and what passengers have come to expect from their airlines.

"Flying any other way will become archaic fast." George added, as he observed the business passengers entering an aircraft on it's way to New York, loading minutes before departure time.

"The old system treats everyone the same. We at Meridian automatically recognize, in a non-intrusive fashion, the unique needs of each and every passenger in the Meridian Club. By doing so, we have almost completely eliminated the bottlenecks that cause delays. Once the passenger's face is identified upon entering the terminal gates, we can link that to our data warehouse which has everything we need to know about the passenger to optimize their flight experience and time spent traveling. Not only that, the Meridian Terminal in LAX is one of the safest in the world. Since it is directly linked to every criminal database in the world, records can be spotted immediately for convicted felons and terrorists. Of course, we have no access to misdemeanor or drug charges for privacy reasons."

The airport is exclusively designed for the convenience of the customer: the passenger. The airline, which occupies the space at the airport, caters directly to every need of the passenger. The car and helicopter service ensure minimum travel time to the airport. Once inside the airport, a Meridian representative is present to assist the passenger with anything he or she may need to get directly to the door of their flight. Baggage is kept with the passenger at all times, with the exception of extremely large bags, which can be checked at the door of the plane. Passengers are permitted to board up until two minutes until departure. Once the passenger is in the airport, the facial recognition technology opens the profile of the passenger, permitting them to proceed past large gates into the terminals, as opposed to the metal detector lines and baggage x-ray belts with size restrictions on baggage being brought into the terminal. The facial recognition scan also alerts the gate that the passenger is on his or her way, checking that passenger in. There is an additional facial recognition point at the entrance of the plane, confirming the passenger has entered the aircraft. The seats are catered to the business traveler as well. For the smaller commutes in the Meridian Jets, the traveler has a personalized travel experience, including full docking station for laptops, printers, fax machines, and an FCC approved cell phone repeater that allows the passenger to stay in communication at all times during the flight. Personalized movie and dinner selections are available as well and can be selected before the flight. For the longer flights, cross continental over 9 hours, the seats are extended and equipped with dividers to provide a suite-like atmosphere for privacy.

But how has George Bunching made millions just 'doing his job?' The side-by-side fund and direct investing has allowed him to take personal investments in the spinouts. But don't be fooled. He has made Airoecraft even more. Their investment returns from spinouts surpassed revenues this year, not profits, but revenues. Meridian is on a path to profitability in less than nine months as their revenues continue to increase 10 fold since their inception.

The future looks bright for the airplane manufacturer and even brighter for their CIO. The airline price war and saga may continue for now, but not for long. Thanks to George and his vision of affordable and safe elite airline travel made possible through Meridian, the paradigm of airline travel has been changed forever, never to return to the unreliability and hassles of air travel normalcy.

Chapter 10

Implications of the Future Corporation

The evolution of information technology corporations toward the model described in Chapter 6 will affect the capital markets, how corporate R&D is managed, how product development organizations are run, how contributors are compensated, how benefits are administered, and the lifestyles of people involved in the industry. Because the information technology industry is accounting for a growing portion of the US economy (close to 9% of the private non-farm Gross Domestic Product in 2001, and 28% to 42% of the Gross Domestic Income annual growth since 1995),[64] these changes will, to some degree, effect the whole country.

---

64 US Department of Commerce *The Emerging Digital Economy II*, Washington, D.C. (1999) and US National Science Foundation *Science and Engineering Indicators 2000*, Washington, D.C. (2000).

The Effects on the Capital Markets

The leading edge corporations who transition to the new model first will become much more attractive investments, exhibiting lower risks and higher returns than their old-style competitors. This will accelerate the shift of capital towards those companies, setting up a virtuous cycle from the investor's standpoint. The more companies make the transition, the more the rest will be under pressure to do the same in order to attract the capital that they need to satisfy their shareholders' requirements. Mature information technology companies who are not willing to make the transition could become candidates for a 1980's style leveraged buy-out or a 1990's style boardroom revolution. As was the case with many of the integrated film studios,[65] once a mature information technology company is bought out, the new owners will find that they can quickly increase the market value of what they bought by doing the necessary structural changes to make the company a competitive distribution company.

I realize that this goes against the conventional wisdom that information technology companies do not make good LBO targets. But that conventional wisdom is already under attack. Tom Gores' Platinum Equity has done over 30 LBOs in the technology sector since 1995, including both information technology hardware and software companies, making Gores a cool $1 billion according to Forbes Magazine's estimate. Gores' approach with his acquisitions is to cut product development and production expenditures and build up their services business.

The boardroom revolution is back as well: in 2001, Sam Wyly and his brother George launched a hostile takeover of Computer Associates (CA), one of the four largest software companies. The takeover method included a proxy battle to replace the founder and Chairman as well as a number of other board members. Interestingly, CalPERS was the first institutional

---

65 Richard E. Caves *Creative Industries,* Boston: HBS Press (2000), pg. 95.

investor who let it be known that it would back Wyly's bid.[66] The bid did not succeed, but Sam Wyly said that he would continue using his family-controlled hedge fund Ranger Capital Group to invest in other companies with poor management and agitate for change. [67]

As the institutional investors begin to see improving financial results from transformed information technology corporations, they will force the same transitions upon other industry sectors that share similar characteristics such as technology-driven disruptive change and an active venture-funded startup scene.

The Effects on Corporate R&D

Corporate research will continue to play a critical role in the creation and commercialization of new technology. Although some portion of the new technology generated from the corporate research lab will find its way into follow-on releases and products, a significant focus will become creating the breakthrough technologies that disrupt current markets. Breakthrough technology will need to be incubated into startup companies that will need to be spun out and financed via venture capital.

Some corporate research labs will be better off operating independently, spun out from their corporate parents. An excellent example of how an independent corporate research lab should work can be found in Sarnoff Corporation. Founded in 1942 as RCA Laboratories, it is famous for having invented (in 1950) the color picture tube or CRT; today's color TV system in 1951; the liquid crystal display (LCD) in 1968; and much of the basic technology behind America's new digital and high-definition television (HDTV) system, launched in 1997. In 1951 the facility was renamed in honor of RCA Chairman General David Sarnoff. In 1986 General Electric bought RCA, and sold off its television business in 1987

---

66 *Wall Street Journal,* (August 21, 2001).
67 *Wall Street Journal,* (August 31, 2001).

to Thomson, a French electronics company. Sarnoff Labs was sold to SRI International at the same time, becoming a for-profit subsidiary of SRI, a not-for-profit contract research company.

By 1992, Sarnoff had successfully converted itself from a lab dependent on corporate sponsorship into a contract research company, with enough revenue from government and corporate contracts to cover its costs. But Curt Carlson and Norman Winarsky of Sarnoff had become convinced that spinning off companies could create great value for Sarnoff, while the contract research model would never earn more than a 2–3% return, and hence was an insufficient model for a for-profit company. Jim Carnes, the President and CEO of Sarnoff, accepted the leadership to make Sarnoff a venture creation engine. Their first spinout was Sensar, a company formed to commercialize Sarnoff's iris-recognition technology. The Sensar spinout showed that it could be done. The result revolutionized the Sarnoff business model, turning Sarnoff into a spinout engine that by 2001 had created 20 spinouts employing 673 people.[68] [69]

Starting in 1993, Sarnoff put a spinout process in place designed to create startup companies based on Sarnoff technology without losing the Sarnoff researchers in the process. What they did was hire a management and technology team from outside of Sarnoff to commercialize a particular technology. In order to profit from its intellectual property, and to keep its researchers happy, Sarnoff negotiated an equity share in every spinout. Five percent of that equity share is spread to all Sarnoff employees. The key contributors to a particular spinout were allowed to divide up another 20 percent of Sarnoff's share. Thus Sarnoff's researchers could build equity in a portfolio of companies and share in the financial gains of the startups that their inventions created.

---

68 Port, Otis "SRI and Sarnoff: Research Labs Reborn as Spin-Off Machines." *Business Week*, (August 1998).

69 *www.sarnoff.com*

With each new spinout, the Sarnoff spinout process was improved to take into account what had been learned in the last spinout. For example, the processes and systems put into place initially to attempt to keep researchers at Sarnoff were found to cause problems for both the researchers and the venture capitalists. So they were modified to allow the key researchers to move into the spun out startups, when it was found to be in the best interest of Sarnoff.

In 2000 Sarnoff formalized the spinout practices that it had learned into a self-funded, wholly owned subsidiary called nVention, with Norman Winarsky as the President. nVention's initial area of emphasis was on the next generation Internet, with a specific focus on broadband multimedia, connected devices, and smart services. In December 2000 the focus was broadened to include non-Internet spinouts. Sarnoff's parent, SRI, who's CEO was Curt Carlson (since 1998), decided in 2001 to implement the nVention business model to commercialize SRI's research as well.

The Effects on Product Development Organizations

Product development will evolve into two separate disciplines: one oriented toward new-to-the-world product development, and the second for follow-on release development. New product development will be financed differently, staffed differently, controlled differently, and compensated differently than follow-on product development. The two types of development will be done by different types of corporate entities, each specialized in the specific disciplines required to succeed at their specific charters.

New-to-the-world product development will be done by startup companies funded by venture capital. The startups will either be independently created or spinouts of the corporate parent, with the parent retaining some ownership via a venture fund. Follow-on product development will be done either by wholly owned business units or partially owned subsidiaries. Partial ownership will, in general, be the better alternative, since it allows the unit to increase revenue and profitability and reduce unit costs by selling the product into markets (both geographic and industries) not covered by the parent. In addition, the independence from the parent will encourage the parent to seek other sources of competitive products to fill out their offerings.

The Effects on Compensation

It is well known to managers of information technology R&D that the best employees are worth a lot more than the average employee is. Measurements of error-free software code production have produced multiples of as high as 20 times. Even 20 times may be low in creative endeavors, where a creative employee will produce a result that his or her uncreative counterpart is incapable of. The problem in the corporate compensation systems that were established in the 1940's and were thought to be the normal way of compensating employees by the 1960's is that they are unable to differentiate compensation to anything close to this degree. Spreads of compensation of 2x are thought radical. If an average software engineer is paid $70,000 per year, and a top engineer is 20 times as productive, the top engineer is underpaid if he or she is paid less than $1.4 million per year! Corporate compensation systems have trouble with the notion of paying the top engineer even $140,000 per year (i.e. 2x).

In actuality, the situation is even more extreme. All engineering managers know that 20 people do not produce 20 times as much product as one person, because of the inefficiencies involved in communication and coordination among the group of 20. So a single engineer who can produce the same amount of code as 20 average engineers is more productive than a group of 20 average engineers, and is actually worth even more than 20 times their salaries.

The venture-backed startup environment that grew up in the 1980's and 1990's offers an alternative to the best, most creative computer and communications hardware and software designers. Although their base pay and benefits may actually be lower in the startup, stock ownership and options allow the creative designer to command a pay that is *directly linked to the value of the products that he or she designs.* Top engineers, involved with successful startups, can and do get total compensation that matches their relative value to the shareholder, which can even exceed $1.4 million per year.

The Effects on Lifestyles

New product development by the integrated information technology companies will be replaced with the system called in the film industry "flexible specialization"[70]. In this new system, most of the talent and resources will be assembled only in one-shot developments, coordinated by an entrepreneur and financed by venture capitalists. Individuals working in this segment of the information technology industry will live much differently than the employees of current large information technology corporations. They will choose which projects to start themselves or get involved with. When a project is underway, it will likely be all-consuming. But there will be both planned and unplanned gaps of inactivity between projects. Reputations will be critical. Specialization will flourish. Training and keeping up with new technology will be a personal responsibility. Although for some this may seem a very insecure lifestyle, for others it will allow a level of freedom and control over their own lives that they did not have in the corporate world, as well as enormous opportunities for financial success.

For those seeking the more secure and managed corporate world, the distribution companies due to their improved stability will offer that to a degree that today's integrated information technology companies cannot.

---

70 Richard E. Caves *Creative Industries,* Boston: HBS Press (2000), pg. 95

These individuals will find support services and follow-on product development a stable form of employment, with clear career paths, etc.

From a geographic standpoint, clustering will certainly continue to play a significant role. Communities that have a critical mass of the needed specialties, plus proximity to distribution companies, research and educational facilities will be much more likely to hatch successful startups than communities lacking this type of critical mass. Community development officials will need to take this into account. On the other hand, many of the specialists will find that geography is immaterial to them, and that they can exercise their specialty on an international basis "virtually" from a home base of their choice. These "virtual" specialists will seek out high quality of life areas with excellent transportation facilities and broadband communication infrastructures.

The Effects on Benefits

The current corporate benefit structure is built around the assumption of lifetime employment with a single company. The world that the information technology industry is converting to will have to make the assumption that most people will move frequently between employers, with gaps of inactivity (planned and unplanned) in between. For some, retirement will be the same lifestyle that they earned the right to live before "retirement", but simply with less frequent projects with longer gaps in between projects. For most people this will be a much more fulfilling type of "retirement" than the version it will replace. From a financial standpoint it also will be much less stressful, because most of the information technology workers will have earned incomes up until they are incapacitated.

Clearly, this requires that health insurance and retirement savings transfer from the responsibility of the employer to that of the individual. Individuals will need portable health and pension systems that move with the individual from employer to employer, and can survive gaps of employment. The Teachers Insurance and Annuity Association (TIAA) was created in the 1920's to give college professors in US colleges and universities portable insurance and retirement plans, recognizing the fact that a professor's career assumed multiple changes of employers. It is by all accounts an excellent system that has served its constituents well, and should be the model for what information technology professionals should have access to. In fact, information technology professionals should become a new market for TIAA. What is needed is an equivalent portable insurance system offering health insurance. Health savings plans that include disaster insurance are a promising start, but they need to be opened up to all employers, big and small.

Summary

The transformation of the information technology industry will have lasting effects on compensation, benefits, industrial R&D, the capital markets, and lifestyles. As in similar transformations—film industry in the 1940's and 1950's and the restructuring of US business in general in the 1980's and 1990's—people will adapt. The transformations will present opportunities that would otherwise not exist. Those able to take advantage of them will do well.

Chapter 11

Actions for You to Take Today

We are only in the first act of the information age revolution. Accelerating advances in computers, software, and communications are changing the world. As we have seen, the old business structures are not serving us well in this time of rapid technological change, and new structures will have to be put in their place. These changes produce turmoil, both in the businesses involved, and in the stock markets. Turmoil produces discomfort, fear, and dislocations, but it also produces unusual opportunities for those who figure out where things are headed and act based upon that.

What actions should you take now? It depends on who you are and what role you are playing:

The Investor

The market turmoil surrounding the information technology industry has made successful stock picking much more difficult than it was in the 1990's. Almost all of the investment rules that were then taken as gospel have now been dispelled. The "buy and hold" and "invest in excellent companies" rules have been proven wrong by the entrenched communications companies such as Cisco, Lucent, and Nortel, who are now looking riskier than some of their startup competitors. Momentum investing has turned out to be a great way to become poor as many stocks in hot information technology companies dropped by 80–90%. IPO's no longer have the "pop" that they once did as many move quickly down (instead of up) from their initial offering price. Internet companies turned out to be another way to become poor. Value investing focused on finding "under-priced" stocks run the danger of finding the losers who are "under-priced" for good reason: they are going out of business or will shrink forever as almost all of the computer industry leaders did in the 1980's. Junk bond portfolios are full of telecommunications bonds, some of which will never be repaid. The first half of 2001 saw $14 billion in defaulted telecommunications bonds, and that was likely just the tip of the iceberg. Corporate bond portfolios are full of higher-grade telecommunications bonds, many of which are in a continual downgrade process with the danger of ending up as junk.

What should an individual investor do now? The first thing to come to grips with is that the concepts of what is a safe investment and what is a risky investment can change almost overnight in industries going through disruptive change. This includes all information technology stocks: telecommunications services, telecommunications equipment, data communications equipment, computers, software, and Internet related. AT&T once looked as safe as any stock in the world, but now it looks scary and out of control. Cisco thought it was immune to the communications industry problems, but it was not: on April 6, 2001 Cisco's stock sank to

$13.63 on a 30% drop in sales for the first quarter of 2001. Thirteen months earlier, it had been $82. IBM is not immune, although its shift toward being primarily a services company will buffer it more than the pure hardware and software producers. Microsoft is not immune, either.

On the other hand, the companies that change their structures so that they can take advantage of the disruptions will do very well, and will turn into some of the greatest investment opportunities in history. The information technology industry will continue to provide most of the growth in the highly developed economies of the world. Investment portfolios that avoid the sector will run a grave risk of under-performing the stock market in general.

How to pick the winners from the losers? Companies who come the closest to matching the structure outlined in Chapter 6 will have a better shot at innovative new products, better access to capital, and lower cost structures than their competitors. If everything else were equal, they would win. But everything else is not equal. Financial controls, market coverage, leadership, quality control, development processes, and customer service matter as well. Look for the large, well-thought-of information technology companies who are actively converting to a distribution company model, i.e. who are bolstering a strong sales and services operation and divesting their product business units in favor of integrating the best of the startups. Those showing real progress at turning their research lab into a startup spinout factory should be particularly favored. Taken together, these factors will distinguish a winning distribution company from a loser.

Evaluating a winning startup is best left to the professionals, the venture capitalists. They not only have the relevant experience but also get personally involved in maximizing the probability of success. Most individuals who meet the "qualified investors" criteria (usually $200,000 per year income or $1 million net worth) are best off to invest in fund-of-funds that in turn invest in venture capital funds. Very wealthy families will continue to invest in venture capital funds directly—they have the professional investors on their staffs to do a good job of it.

The Information Technology Company CEO

CEOs of Battelle, Cisco, IBM, Nortel, Sarnoff, and SRI: congratulations—you are on the right course. Some of you have taken actions to bolster your distribution and services capabilities, divest some of your traditional product units, and acquire the most innovative startups. Battelle, Sarnoff, and SRI have seriously refocused their research on creating spinouts and recruited venture capitalist to become directly involved.

But none of you are close to the end state. Your main enemy is going to be speed of execution of the transition: the faster the transition, the lower the risk and the better the competitive positioning. Those who get there first will win. Some who have not started yet will pass those who linger.

The CIO

You are one of the major beneficiaries of this industry transformation. Costs will decrease, especially in communications services and equipment where vertical integration is still entrenched. The variety of products will increase substantially with the increase in innovation and breakdown of oligopolies. Compatibility will also increase, as the industry switches increasingly toward customer-driven standards and away from vendor-driven standards. The variety of services available will also increase as the distribution companies increasingly focus on services.

You have the opportunity to use the spinout paradigm to transform your most promising internal systems into stand-alone companies, as the fictional George Bunching did in Chapter 9. In addition to giving your shareholders another source of value creation, this will allow you to cut costs while still obtaining the services that you need. Not only can you share the ongoing operational costs of your custom applications with other customers, but also by releasing your system as a product for all, you can establish industry standards allowing you to avoid future conversion costs. In addition, the opportunity to be part of a spinout will improve your recruiting ability for excellent talent.

The CFO

You will have a critical role to play in transforming your company into the distribution company model. In addition to the divestitures, reorganizations, and acquisitions that will be required to create a leading distribution company, you will also have to implement appropriate processes, controls and procedures to effect spinouts and spin-ins of startups. Fortunately there already are a large number of specialized firms that you can contract help from. To these will be added specialists in the startup spinout and spin-in processes.

The LBO Fund Manager

If the history of the integrated film studios is any guidance, the management of the integrated information technology companies may also be less than nimble in restructuring their companies into distribution companies. This will present opportunities for those of you focusing on information technology LBOs (yes, there are a few of you), who will be able to privatize these companies, split off the operations that are unnecessary for their core distribution and services function, and then take them public again realizing significant profits. This could become one of the hot LBO areas of the early 21st century.

The Business Unit Manager

The conversion to a distribution company structure will allow you to focus your business unit on what it does best, expand your horizontal markets, gain increased autonomy, and implement the culture, controls, processes and systems that make the most sense for the unit. Nirvana!

Everyone will benefit, including the parent distribution company and the product business units, not to mention the shareholders and customers.

Your first step is to meet with the head of Product Line Marketing and your CEO to come to an agreement per product regarding the degree of exclusivity required by the distribution company in the markets it addresses. The degree of exclusivity required for current and follow-on products will guide what percentage ownership the distribution company should keep in your business unit. Keeping majority ownership is probably unnecessary and non-optimal, and may not sit well with the new investors in the spun-out business unit. But if there is a desire to maintain exclusive reseller relationships in a number of the products in a number of markets, some ownership may be useful.

The next step is to determine if the business unit should spin out as a single company, or as multiple companies. If the business unit consists of multiple products or product lines that do not share many manufacturing or development resources, multiple spinouts should be seriously considered. That would allow the new companies to focus their systems, culture, contracts, etc. even more specifically on a particular product, without having to worry about the effects on other products or product lines. Each spinout would be free to strike their own deals regarding exclusivity with the parent distribution company, as well as work out plans to address their own horizontal market expansion. Economies of scale need not be effected, since the spinouts can gain them by converting to contract manufacturing and outsourcing other functions to specialist firms.

The final step is to develop a plan for addressing the new horizontal markets for the products. Even the largest distribution company cannot address all markets in all geographic areas for a particular product. In the integrated companies, the effect is that many markets are left unaddressed, forsaking revenue potential. Once separated, your spun-out product business units can much more effectively pursue horizontal markets for their products, striking distribution and reseller agreements with whomever can provide coverage in each market. Their new distribution partners do not have to fear, as they may well have with the integrated company, that the business unit's parent will grab the market away from them once they develop it. Many spun-off business units will find that they can double their sales, and improve their competitive positioning against horizontal competitors. The resulting increase in unit volumes will benefit the former parent distribution company as well, since it should be able to obtain better pricing due to the reduction in unit costs.

The Information Technology Professional

The most creative of you have the opportunity of gaining super star status, with compensation to match. As a member of the *A List*, you will be courted to be on the teams of new startups, and your reputation and fame will raise the value of the ventures you are associated with. Annual compensation in the millions will be normal for the members of the *A List*, most of it derived from stock option exercises. To play, you will have to become a proven player in startups, leaving the corporate or university lab where you may currently be employed. You will need to develop a track record of creating successful new-to-the-world products, pulling together the entrepreneurial team and financing to commercialize it, establishing the market for it, and then transferring it successfully to a distribution company. Do that a few times, and your name will be golden.

The Entrepreneur

Think of your information technology startup as David, Inc. Don't grow up. Stay small. Pass the baton when the time is at hand to distribute on a wide scale, and pass it to the one or ten companies who are best suited to distribute and evolve it. Then start again, and again, and again. Why chance the dangerous path of transforming yourself into a giant when you don't need to? Why not do what you do best: move fast, recognize an opportunity in the market and go for it. Hire when you need to, fire when you need to. Address markets that don't exist or are new.

Maneuver your business plan on a dime; enter into a market and then learn what is needed to be successful; maintain the freedom to pursue any area of potential profitability; foster a highly creative environment when it is most desperately needed. You can risk it—there is no corporate reputation at risk and you can take on more legal risk than your giant counterpart. You have no customer pressure to stay with the current product line; actually, you don't have any current product line to defend at all. You have no manufacturing capacity to fill, and no talent base to be allocated. Grow your markets fast without being encumbered by the barricades or decision-making bureaucracy of your counterpart. Operate where he does not dare to go: in areas of high uncertainty, in fast growing or undefined markets, with risky technology. Stay small and succeed.

The Graduating Student

Congratulations. You have the opportunity to enter one of the most exciting industries at one of its most exciting moments. Information technology is changing the world and creating its future, and will continue to do so for many years to come. The opportunities are truly limitless. If that is what you are looking for, get on board as quickly as possible.

The startup world will offer the highest rewards if you are truly a creative high achievers. A good sense of self-confidence, self-sufficiency, curiosity, adventure, humor, and ability to solve tough problems will be required for survival. Be prepared for very hard work, long hours, constant disruptions, relocations, failures, layoffs, redirections, firings, and bankruptcies. It all goes with the terrain.

On the other hand, if you do not have much tolerance for change, disruption, being laid off, having to keep your skills constantly up-to-date, or working almost constantly, seek out employment with one of the distribution companies. Although you will find that your income potential is more limited than in the startup world, you will enjoy much better stability of employment, well-defined career paths, and an excellent opportunity to learn the industry.

About the Author

As a technology visionary and information technology industry executive, Reid McRae Watts has built a 25-year career around his love for technology and innovation inside the corporate world. Until his exposure to the venture capital methods for commercializing new-to-the-world innovations, Reid was forced to accept the reality that corporations were not as skilled as startups at bringing those technologies to the public. As he continued his attempts at commercializing such technologies within the corporate environment, his failures ascertained his theory that it simply cannot be done. With an enlightened perspective added to his comprehensive technology background, Reid discovered the real reasons behind the corporate defeats that are haunting the newspaper business sections each week, as well as a solution that utilizes the strengths and weaknesses of the corporation and the startup, uniting them to ensure a successful future of technology.

It is because of Reid's unusually varied exposure to the corporate R&D environment and the venture capital industry that he is able to propose a solution that addresses the root of the problem: the inevitable and unchangeable paradoxes between a startup company and a large corporation that will never allow a corporation to beat the startup in certain innovation projects. Reid has spent 25 years working in large corporate R&D environments, such as in Bell Labs, AT&T, and NCR, with some of the key technologies of our era attempting to commercialize breakthrough innovations. Reid headed the Comten Business Unit at NCR, served on the board of directors of the Microelectronics and Computer Technology Corporation (MCC), and has worked closely with Amdahl, Battelle, Digital Equipment, Cray, Sun, Cisco, Alcatel, Motorola, IBM, as well as a number of smaller high technology companies. As a Vice President of New Ventures at NCR, he implemented a startup incubator and venture fund within a traditional company, and learned why this usually does not work, as well as what actually does. Reid founded Progeny Ventures, LLC, a venture capital management company that has a unique mission and structure to assist mature corporations with early-stage information technology spinouts. Reid serves on the Core Technology Advisory Board of the Battelle Memorial Institute, the largest US contract research company and the operator of four of the US Department of Energy national labs.

Reid has a Masters in Computer Science from the University of Kansas and is a graduate of the executive management programs at Yale and INSEAD (France). He has founded four companies and has been awarded three patents to date. Reid grew up in Switzerland, and has lived in the United States, Beirut, Lebanon and Rome, Italy.

Glossary

Acquisition (ch.2 and ch.6) A purchase. In this book, the word acquisition is used to mean the purchase of all of the equity (outstanding stock) of one company by another. Acquisitions can be paid for in cash, or stock, or a combination of both.

Alto Workstation (ch.1) A prototype precursor of the current day PC, Apple, and SUN workstation, created at Xerox Palo Alto Research Center (PARC) in the 1970's.

Breakthrough Product (ch.4) A product that either is new-to-the-world, or offers substantially better cost/performance than existing products. Note that most products considered "new" are actually new versions of existing products. Breakthrough products create new markets, change the competitive landscape, and undermine existing markets.

Breakthrough Innovation (ch.5 and ch.8) Innovation, usually based on technological breakthroughs, that lead to breakthrough products.

Business Unit or BU (ch.8 and ch.11) An organization within a corporation that operates similar to a wholly owned business with its own profit and loss statements and decision making. *Also see* Decentralized Corporate Structures.

Capital Markets (ch.10) Markets where capital is raised by corporations. This includes the stock markets, private equity markets, and bond markets.

Carried Interest (ch.5) The share (oftentimes 20%) of profits from the sale or liquidation of an investment portfolio that is allocated to the general partners of a venture capital partnership. The purpose of carried interest is to link the compensation of the general partners with the success of the investment portfolio, motivating them to maximize the investor's (limited partner's) returns.

Cell Switching (ch.1) A form of packet switching that uses relatively short, fixed-length packets. First incorporated in Bell Labs' Datakit prototype in the early 1980's. Appeared later in a set of products from various vendors known as Asynchronous Transfer Mode (ATM). A key underlying technology of today's broadband networks.

Centralized Corporate Structure (ch.5 and ch.8) In centralized corporate structures, profit and loss decision making is centralized at the senior management level, in the extreme at the CEO level. The costs and revenues of the company are accumulated together across the whole company and brought into balance at the top level. *Also see* Decentralized Corporate Structure.

Circuit Switching (ch.1) The original approach for making dial-up telephone connections. Results in a circuit being established between the calling and receiving telephones, meaning that the telephone network allocates a specific amount of bandwidth (typically 56 or 64 K bits/sec) to the call for the duration of the call, regardless of whether it is being used or not. The original circuit switches were pegboards with human operators who actually made electrical connections between the telephones involved in a call. Those were replaced by electro-mechanical switches (called step-by-step switches) that automated the peg board operations. Electro-mechanical switches gave way to computer-controlled switches, still making mechanical contacts, which became Electronic Switching Systems

(ESS). The digital switches that first started to appear in the 1970's no longer made an electrical connection between the telephones, but still allocated a fixed amount of digital bandwidth to each circuit (64 K bits/second, to be precise), and hence continued be referred to as circuit switches.

Commercialization (ch.1) Exploitation for profit. In this book, the word "commercialization" is invariably linked to turning a new technology into a product or service that can be sold at a profit.

Compression Algorithms (ch.3) A software program that reduces the number of bytes in transmitted or stored data. Upon receipt (in the case of transmitted data) or retrieval (in the case of stored data), the data is "decompressed" into its original state. Compression algorithms take advantage of the fact that a lot of data is replicated.

Cookie Cutter Structure (ch.6) In this book, cookie cutter structure refers to corporate organization charts that look structurally so similar to each other that one is reminded of the similarity of cookies made from a cookie cutter.

Corporate Raider (ch.2) An individual who attempts to gain control of a public company in order to reorganize it and replace its management. *Also see* Leveraged Buyout.

Corporate Culture (ch.5) The value system of a corporation. Includes what is rewarded, what is punished, values of the leaders, etc.

Corporate Venture Capital (ch.5) Corporate investment in venture-backed startups. The startups can be either spinouts from the corporation or of independent origin. Corporations either invest in startups out of their general corporate funds or allocate specific funds for this purpose.

Cross-Licenses (ch.8) An agreement between two corporations to license their patent portfolios to each other.

Decision Gate (ch.4) A pre-defined point in the product development process where a decision is made to proceed or not to proceed with the development of the product.

Decentralized Corporate Structure (ch.5) Corporations with decentralized structures have Business Units that have Profit and Loss decision making responsibilities. The Business Units are run as individual businesses, and roll up their own costs and revenues. *Also see* Centralized Corporate Structure.

Distributor or Distribution Company (ch.5 and ch.6) A company that takes a product from a manufacturer and distributes it to the buyers, either directly or via a retailers. Many distributors add service offerings to the products being distributed (e.g. help desk, repair, professional services) so that they can offer their customers complete solutions.

Downsizing (ch.5) Cutting the operational costs of a company by laying off staff.

Ethernet (ch.1) The first commercially successful local area network (LAN), invented by Xerox Palo Alto Research in the 1970's, and first incorporated in the Alto Workstation. The original version of Ethernet used a shared coaxial cable with multiple connections.

Equity (ch.10) A risk interest or ownership right in property, usually in the form of stock.

Fang Connector (ch.1) An Ethernet connector that clamped to the shared coaxial Ethernet cable and inserted a "fang" into the cable's core to make the connection.

Fiber (ch.1) Glass, elongated into long, thin bendable strands. The thickness of a light fiber strand is less than a human hair. Signals are sent down a fiber by pulsing a laser at the transmitting end.

Firewall (ch.1) In computer networks, a firewall is a special-purpose computer that is placed between the internal corporate network and external public networks such as the Internet. The firewall carefully monitors what goes between them, to prevent viruses and objectionable material from entering the corporate network, and prevent sensitive corporate information from being accessed from the public network. A firewall can also collect information that can be used to catch intruders or "hackers" attempting to breach network security.

Hawthorne Effect (ch.5) The temporary improvement in worker productivity that results from making the workers part of a productivity experiment or process change. The effect was first noticed in the Hawthorne plant of Western Electric. Production increased not as a consequence of actual changes in working conditions introduced by the plant's management, but rather because management demonstrated interest in such improvements.

Hurdle Rate (ch.8) A preset rate that must be achieved in a business plan for a corporation to invest in the plan. Hurdle rates are often set on the Return on Investment, Break Even Time, and amount of revenue that must be produced in a set period of time.

Hot Product Company (ch.6) Successful startups who have their initial success because of a single "hot" product that they developed.

Impatient Capital (ch.2, ch.5 and ch.6) Capital for which the investors want returns in the current year or even current quarter. Returns can be in income or appreciation of the investment. All institutional capital, whether mutual funds, insurance, or pension funds, where the investment manager is measured on quarterly and annual performance, is impatient capital.

Information Technology or IT (ch.3 and ch.6) Information technology includes computers, terminals, routers, modems, software, PCs, servers, mainframes, storage devices, microprocessors, telephone equipment, switching systems, fiber optic devices, transmission systems, etc. In short, everything associated with the computer, software, and telecommunications industries.

Internet (ch.1), a.k.a. "The Net," the Internet was first set up by the Defense Advanced Research Project Agency (DARPA) in the early 1980's to interconnect existing research networks at universities and research labs. In the mid-1990's it was turned over to private companies to operate, and was opened up to allow commercial activity and sites (the ".com" sites).

Internal Incubation (ch.5 and ch.8) Incubation refers to the process of creating a new startup. It includes hiring the senior management, creating the business plan, doing the market analysis, creating the legal structures, and initial funding (so called "seed funding"). Internal incubation refers to a corporation incubating startups inside of the parent corporation.

Intellectual Property (ch.5 and ch.8) Non-physical assets of a corporation, including software, engineering designs, and patents owned by the company.

IPO (ch.2) Initial Public Offering. An IPO converts a private company into a public company by selling stock shares on a public exchange.

Leveraged Buyout or LBO (ch.2 and ch.11) In a leveraged buyout, an individual or group of investors buy out the owners of a public corporation using borrowed money. The result of an LBO is the conversion of a public company into a private one. Private equity funds that specialize in LBOs are call LBO Funds. *Also see* Corporate Raider.

Liquidate (ch.6) The conversion of an asset into cash via a sale. Venture capitalists refer to liquidity events when they either IPO or sell via a private sale one of their startups.

Mergers and Acquisitions or M&A (ch.5) Refers to the activities involved in one corporation buying another.

Magnetic Disk Capacity (ch.3) Magnetic disks include both hard drives and floppies or diskettes. Capacity is measured in the number of bytes stored per disk, usually in units of megabytes (millions of bytes), gigabytes (billions of bytes), or terabytes (trillions of bytes).

Mainframe Computer (ch.1) Computers that occupy whole rooms. Mainframes often require special power and cooling plant in order to operate. Mainframes were the predominant form of computers before the arrival of minicomputers in the 1970's. Minicomputers or "minis" were designed to fit in a closet, lab, or office, using normal electrical power and built-in air-cooling. Personal Computers became the predominant form of computer in the late 1980's. Mainframe computers still exist and are sold by IBM, Hitachi, Fujitsu and Unisys, although they account for a constantly shrinking market share. Minicomputers were renamed servers with the advent of the client-server computing paradigm in the 1980's.

Market Capitalization (ch.1) The value of a public corporation assigned to it by the stock market. A company's market capitalization can be calculated by multiplying the number of shares outstanding by the current market price of those shares.

Matrix Management (ch.4) An organization structure with both rows and columns, indicating that some people report to more than one superior. Typically in a matrixed organization, the "columns" are functional departments such as engineering, manufacturing, procurement, etc., while the "rows" are projects led by project leaders.

Moore's Law (ch.3) A prediction, made by Gordon Moore in 1965, that the density of computer circuitry on a chip would double every 12 months, creating an exponential increase in computer power. In 1995 he updated his law to doubling every 24 months.

New Product Development Cycle (ch.6) The cycle that corporations go through in developing new products. The cycle starts with a concept proposal and ends with everything in place to manufacture, distribute, market, sell, and support the product.

New-to-the-world Products (ch.6, ch.8 and ch.10) In this book, new products that are not simply new versions of existing products are called new-to-the-world products. *Also see* Sequels.

Outsource (ch.4) To source or purchase a service from outside of the corporation. Outsourced activities extend from the operation of the company cafeteria, to manufacturing, legal services, human resource services, accounting services, etc.

Packet Switching (ch.1) An approach to transmitting chunks or "packets" of information from one computer to another. Each packet contains the address of where it is being sent to, and each computer along the way routes it based on that address. Packet switching was invented in the 1960's for computer networks, but it was not until local area networks and the Internet arrived in the 1980's that it became accepted. Even in the early 1990's it still was being dismissed as not being appropriate for business critical applications. But by the end of the 1990's, it was clear to all that packet switching was fated to replace circuit switching for all applications.

Patient Capital (ch.2, ch.5, ch.6 and ch.8) Capital for which the investor is willing to wait five to ten years to obtain any return, including the original investment. All venture capital is patient capital.

Phantom World (ch.5) In this book, this term refers to corporations attempting to emulate the venture-backed startup world inside of their corporations, creating "phantom" stocks, stock options, carried interest, and boards of directors.

Product Line Management or PLM (ch.8) An organization with a corporation that manages the planning and marketing associated with an entire product line.

Private Equity (ch.2) Stock that is not actively traded on a public market such as the NYSE, NASDAQ, etc.

Private Sale (ch.6) The sale of a company to another company, where the former is privately held (i.e. is not traded on a stock market).

Process Management (ch.5) The management of the processes that define a corporation's operations. Included are design processes, manufacturing processes, distribution processes, pay processes, etc.

Processor Speed (ch.3) The speed of the Central Processing Unit (CPU) in a computer. The power of a computer is tied to the speed at which its processing unit is able to carry out instructions such as arithmetic operations. The faster the speed, the more "powerful" the computer.

Puzzle M&A (ch.5) In this book, this term refers to the activities involved in merging two mature corporations where the functions, geographic coverage, and strengths fit together like a jigsaw puzzle.

Public Equity (ch.2) Stock that is actively traded on a public market such as the NYSE, NASDAQ, etc.

Research and Development or R&D (ch.1) The activities associated with the creation of a new product. Research is usually focused on discovering a new scientific principle, or creating a new material, chemical, or algorithm. Development is focused on creating the prototype of a new product (advanced development), and subsequently the engineering drawings, manufacturing specifications, and software for the production of a new product.

Sequels and Follow-on Products (ch.6 and ch.10) The term sequels comes from the cinema film industry, where it refers to a new film that is based on an existing film. In the manufacturing industries, most new products are actually new versions of products that already exist, and hence are referred to as sequels in this book. *Also see* New-To-The-World Products.

Slingshot Syndrome (ch.1 and ch.5) The pattern first established in the computer industry in the 1980's where startups with little resources are able to replace large, established corporations. The syndrome appears to be particularly successful when the markets involved are being disrupted by rapid technological change, putting a premium on rapid commercialization of new technology. The term is derived from the biblical story of David and Goliath where David slayed the arrogant, heavily armored and unsuspecting giant Goliath with a mere slingshot.

Spin-in (ch.6) In this book, spin-in refers to the acquisition of a startup by a mature company.

Spinout (ch.6) A.k.a. spin-off. A spinout is a new corporation created from assets of another company. In this book, spinout always refers to the creation of a startup from the assets of a mature company.

Stable Market (ch.5) A market with a well-defined structure of suppliers and customers, stable pricing, stable demand and supply, and little opportunity for new entrants.

Startup A fledgling business enterprise.

Strategic Spinout (ch.8) A spinout done for the purpose of implementing part of the strategy of the parent company.

Telecommunications Act of 1996 (ch.3) Described by the US Federal Communications Commission (FCC) as the first major overhaul of the Telecommunications Act of 1934, which laid the regulatory groundwork for the telephone industry. The Telecommunications Act of 1996 set up a framework for introducing competition into every aspect of the telephone business, deregulating the carriers as competition is introduced.

Wide Area Network or WAN (ch.3) A data network that extends between buildings, interconnecting Local Area Networks or LANs.

Venture Backed Startup (ch.4) A startup company that is primarily financed by venture capital.

Vertically Integrated (ch.6) A vertically integrated company is one which provides most of the services, parts and materials that it needs from its own internal operations. *See also* Outsourcing.